PREDATOR KING

PREDATOR KING

PETER NYGARD'S DARK LIFE OF RAPE, DRUGS, AND BLACKMAIL

MELISSA CRONIN

foreword by
FMR. FEDERAL PROSECUTOR DAN DORSKY

afterword by
FMR. FBI SPECIAL AGENT MIKE CAMPI

Hot Books

CONTENTS

*They used to say that Nygard is the best secret in town.
Now the secret is out.*

—Peter Nygard

CAST OF CHARACTERS

PETER NYGARD

A Finnish schoolboy turned international "polyester phenom," the fashion designer has been accused of verbal abuse, rape, sex trafficking, and more over the years.

HILKKA NYGARD

Nygard's mother. He was dedicated to her throughout his life and put her up in his Viking Hill estate in the Bahamas and named his yacht, the *Lady Hilkka*, after her.

PIRJO-LIISA NYGARD

Nygard's sister, she was perhaps his closest friend. He was devastated when she passed away in January 2020.

NANCY EBKER

A 1970s fashion designer who said Nygard "ruined" her life through their legal fight over her company.

PATRICIA BICKLE

Nygard's ex, she gave birth to his children Bianca, Alia, and Kai.

HELENA JAWORSKI

Nygard's ex, she gave birth to his son, Peter Jr. and later fought him for child support.

KAARINA PAKKA

Nygard's ex, she asked for Canada's biggest child-support payment ever in Canadian history, at the time.

RICHETTE ROSS

The former house manager at Nygard Cay, she later accused Nygard of raping her.

PERRY CHRISTIE

The Prime Minister of the Bahamas from 2012 to 2017, his administration was tainted over claims of Nygard's corrupt influence.

SHANE GIBSON

The former Immigration Minister of the Bahamas, he received more than $90,000 in payments from Nygard from 2012 to 2013.

SUELYN MEDEIROS

Nygard's longtime "girlfriend," she wrote about her years by his side in her memoir.

MARIDEL CARBUCCIA

A former Nygard employee, she later sued him for sexually assaulting her on the job in his Marina Del Rey home/office.

REVEREND C. B. MOSS

A reverend and community activist in Bain Town, an underprivileged area of Nassau where Nygard often found his young prey.

COURTNEY STODDEN

A model, actress and singer-songwriter, Stodden claims Nygard sexually assaulted her at a red carpet event.

TIME LINE

JULY 24, 1941

Peter Nygard is born in Finland.

JULY 24, 1943

Peter Nygard later claimed that this was his true date of birth.

1944–1945

The Lapland war ravages Nygard's homeland of Finland.

1947

The Nygard family moves to Helsinki.

1952

The Nygard family moves to Deloraine, Manitoba.

1964

Nygard graduates from the University of North Dakota.

1964

Nygard joins Eaton's department store chain in Canada.

1967

Nygard quits his position at Eaton's to join Nathan Jacob's Tan Jay clothing line.

SEPTEMBER 20, 1968

Nygard marries model Carolyn Knight in Winnipeg.

1970

Nygard is full owner of Tan Jay.

1967

The Nygard family moves to Winnipeg.

1973

Nygard meets model Helena Jaworski.

APRIL 21, 1974

Nygard's son Peter is born to Helena Jaworski.

1974

Jaworski begins child-support proceedings against Nygard.

1975

Nygard strikes his controversial deal with designer Nancy Ebker. They would spend roughly a decade in court fighting over her business.

1977

Nygard's daughter Bianca is born to Patricia Bickle.

1979

Nygard's daughter Alia is born.

JANUARY 1980

Nygard arrested for rape

JUNE 1980

Nygard's rape case is stayed after the alleged victim refuses to testify.

1986

Nygard agrees on shared custody with Bickle.

1987

Nygard begins his database of female guests to Nygard Cay.

1988

Nygard's ex-girlfriend Kaarina Pakka begins child-support proceedings against Nygard over their son Mika.

1995

A former Nygard employee sues Nygard for having sex with her "against her will." The case is settled out of court.

JUNE 22, 1996

The *Winnipeg Free Press* publishes an explosive cover story that reveals several former Nygard employees made sexual-harassment complaints against him to the Manitoba Human Rights Commission.

1997 TO 2000

Nygard dates Anna Nicole Smith off and on.

2000

Nygard's ex Kaarina Pakka demands $68,000 per month in child support.

2000

Prince Andrew, Sarah "Fergie" Ferguson, and their daughters Princess Beatrice and Princess Eugenie visit Nygard Cay.

2004

Nygard reaches a child-support agreement with Pakka.

JULY 2004

Nygard is a judge for the "Caribbean Flava Top Model Search."

JULY 2008

Nygard hosts a *Playboy* photo shoot and the "Racey Girl International Swimsuit and Lingerie Model Search Finals" at Nygard Cay.

NOVEMBER 6, 2009

Nygard opens a massive concept store in Times Square.

NOVEMBER 2009

An electrical fire nearly destroys Nygard Cay.

DECEMBER 2009

Nygard files a lawsuit in the US District Court against the CBC, claiming that their uninvited reporter had recorded his restricted event and had therefore performed copyright infringement.

The Nygard International Partnership files an application in San Jose, California, attempting to subpoena Google over a comment on a blog.

APRIL 9, 2010

The CBC series *Fifth Estate* airs the episode "Larger Than Life," all about Peter Nygard.

APRIL 14, 2010

The National Labor Committee issues a press release accusing him of producing his clothes in a Jordanian "sweatshop."

AUGUST 4, 2011

Workers at the Nan Kuang garment factory in Cambodia walk out over poor conditions. Workers reportedly sew clothes for the Nygard lines there.

2012

Nygard files a defamation lawsuit against the CBC.

2012

The PLP party sweeps the Bahamas General Election. Nygard celebrates with a video titled "Nygard Takes Bahamas Back."

2012 TO 2013

Nygard deposits more than $90,000 into the Miami bank account of Bahamas Minister of Immigration and Labor Shane "Shameless" Gibson.

AUGUST 2013

Bahamas Prime Minister Perry Christie announces the Stem Cell Therapy and Research Bill in Parliament.

MARCH 2, 2014

Peter Nygard sexually assaults Courtney Stodden, she claims.

MARCH 2015

Nygard makes a presentation at the St. Kitts Biomedical Research Foundation's Strategy Conference on Reverse Aging Treatments.

2016

The Prime Minister of St. Kitts grants Nygard three rooms at the Joseph N. France General Hospital to begin his stem cell research and treatments.

MAY 2017

The Nygard-backed PLP party is eviscerated in a lopsided landslide election by an electorate fed up with corruption and insider dealings.

JULY 2017

Clean Clothes Campaign announces that workers at a Nygard factory in Cambodia are demanding roughly half a million dollars in back pay.

2018

The US State Department issues a travel advisory for the Bahamas warning tourists that "sexual assault is common" in the island nation.

SEPTEMBER 2018

The Bahamian authorities seize Nygard Cay over Nygard's failure to pay nearly $3 million in legal fees in one lawsuit.

JULY 2019

Allegations of rape by Peter Nygard are made to the Royal Bahamian Police Force.

JANUARY 22, 2020

Former Nygard employee Maridel Carbuccia sues Nygard over sexual-harassment claims.

JANUARY 27 2020

Bahamas newspaper the *Tribune* reports that Nygard has been sued by a female Jane Doe, who claims that he had sex with her against her will at his California home when she was a minor.

JANUARY 31, 2020

Famed attorney Gloria Allred's firm (Allred, Maroko & Goldberg) files an amended complaint on behalf of Carbuccia, going after Nygard for even more.

FEBRUARY 13, 2020

Ten Jane Does file suit against Nygard in New York City for rape and sex trafficking.

FEBRUARY 18, 2020

The lawyers in the NY State Jane Doe suit announced that in the week following the filing of their complaint, they had been contacted by more than one hundred previously unknown victims and/or witnesses to Nygard's sexual predations. These new stories of rape, violence, sodomy, and/or confinement spanned four decades and these new women hailed from Canada, the US, and the Bahamas.

FEBRUARY 22, 2020

The *New York Times* publishes an explosive report about the sexual assault allegations against Nygard, after speaking with more than 250 people.

FEBRUARY 25, 2020

The FBI raids Nygard's New York City headquarters and Marina Del Rey home. By that evening, Dillard's announced it would be cancelling its orders with Nygard. Perhaps in a bid to create distance and save his empire, Nygard announced he would be stepping down from the companies effective immediately.

MARCH 3, 2020

The CBC reports that Nygard has been slapped with legal action by Hollywood mega-mogul Michael Sitrick.

MARCH 6, 2020

The *New York Times* publishes the second story in their Nygard series, detailing the harassment some women claim they endured in reporting the story.

MARCH 10, 2020

The Nygard Group of Companies announces they will be filing "a notice of intention to file a proposal' under the Canadian Bankruptcy and Insolvency Act.

MARCH 11, 2020

The *Winnipeg Free Press* reports that Nygard employees have been directed to preserve all documents.

MARCH 13, 2020

A Canadian judge orders Nygard's companies to pay back a $25 million loan owed to American lenders within seven days.

MARCH 18, 2020

A Canadian judge places several of Nygard's companies into "receivership," which gives full control of the companies and their finances to an outside firm.

PREDATOR KING

FOREWORD

A small subset of the human population are sociopaths. They are not capable of kindness, caring, empathy, guilt, regret, or compassion. They have no conscience. Their sole concern is themselves, and exerting power over others. Sociopaths destroy and wreak havoc on their victims, while they carefully cover their trail. They are nothing but predators.

What might such a monster look like in real life? If these stories are to be believed, then Melissa Cronin paints a comprehensive portrait of Peter Nygard's apparent rotted, sociopathic core. This is a story of what can result when a person simply does not have remorse, compassion, or a conscience. It is beyond tragic. Cronin details Nygard's skilled, unending application of all the well-worn corruptive and brutal levers of power; all to perpetuate his sick terror-filled games played for pleasure and all leading to the destruction of countless young lives—usually via rape—and utilizing threats, bribes, hush money, political payoffs, control over corrupt government and law enforcement, psychological coercion, the false lure of modeling and fashion careers and other false promises, brute force, taking advantage of others' financial desperation, drugs, even the likely killing of a victim's dog. If the charges are true, then underage girls were not safe, and may have been his preferred targets. As one victim put it, still shell-shocked years later: "I told God that I did not know we had these kinds of monsters in this world."

As a former prosecutor, it is a truism that everybody is entitled to the presumption of innocence. Relying on her sources—whose veracity has not yet been tested in a court of law—Cronin argues that Nygard allegedly camouflaged himself behind the facade of decency: a respected businessman, a celebrity, a philanthropist, and charitable donor hosting church groups and children's camps, demonstrating concern for the poor—all draped with admirable public pronouncements about how much he especially valued women and their talents. Under this camouflage, so many victims had no reason to suspect that the smiling, disarming, and dashing fashion executive inviting them to a "pamper party" was in reality a predator intent on inflicting everlasting trauma. Until it was too late. Worse than Epstein, Weinstein, Cosby, and others in what he allegedly did, but like them with an army of well-compensated enablers ensuring that the damage he wreaked continued running seamlessly like a well-oiled machine.

One victim in the book innocently wonders "does he even still have a conscience?" Her question unwittingly misses the point—chillingly, sociopaths, like the Nygard who is portrayed, never had a conscience to lose. As I write during the coronavirus outbreak, if the allegations are true, then I can't help but see the parallels: no way to know that you have come into contact with a destructive virus, without any defense to its assault before it moves on to others through the host, as Nygard apparently did with so many victims by turning them into recruiters for what he allegedly called new "sacrifices."

I recite all of these charges I have read in this book against Nygard of course just as allegations—albeit consistent ones, and made by dozens and dozens of people over the continuing course of decades. But I draw on personal experience as well. Former FBI Agent Mike Campi and I very recently traveled to the Bahamas. What we experienced was staggering. Virtually every single random person we encountered (in every instance we went unannounced and unscheduled), told us that they had direct or secondhand experience with Nygard's orgies. Whether it be vendors, restaurant employees, taxi drivers, community leaders, hotel employees, or religious figures—they said they knew. Some spoke only in whispers. Notably only two, a powerful government figure and a former law enforcement officer in the Bahamas, refused to speak with us.

Most women we spoke with had themselves been invited to Nygard's parties or claimed to know at least one victim. Many promised to have victims reach out to us, but in only one instance was a connection made. It was like a horror film where we opened the door to the basement that everyone knows about but dares not speak of. And what they all had in common was apparent fear. Even with Nygard long off the island and facing arrest warrants, most were unwilling to go on the record. After a few days of this type of inquiry, we were approached one morning by a man who specifically sought us out at the back of our hotel. This was the only time a person had approached us, as in all other cases it was the other way around. He told us that we were barking up the wrong tree and that Nygard was a philanthropist and completely innocent. He had ready "facts" at hand, such as that Bahamian girls would never go to Nygard's estate. Having spoken to numerous and random Bahamians, each of whom told us the exact opposite from personal experience, it seemed obvious to us that he was a plant, sent to misdirect us. The corresponding implication was unavoidable that we were being followed. We became much more cautious from this time forward, and very wary of unwittingly leading whoever was following us to the people who might be willing to talk.

As of this writing, federal authorities recently executed sweeping search warrants of Nygard's homes and businesses on both US coasts. One of his Bahamian estates is now a hostel charging $40 per night for a bunk bed, so the financial pressures must be severe. Perhaps his end is near. From what I've read in the book you are about to read yourselves, and assuming there is truth to the charges, it's far too little too late, but at least it's something. As a former federal prosecutor who prosecuted some of the most significant cases in this country, I would have thoroughly enjoyed bringing this case to justice. When you read this book, you'll understand why.

—Dan Dorsky
Former federal prosecutor
March 2020

AUTHOR'S NOTE

The monster under the bed is real. The boogeyman in the closet. The childish connection with that sense of evil lurking in the darkness is one of the most primal—and accurate—of human instincts.

As an investigative journalist, for nearly twenty years I have worked to find and shine a light on all of the predators that make a home and a hunting ground in the shadows. In 2014, I thought I had found the nightmare king of them all when I began reporting on billionaire pedophile Jeffrey Epstein.

My introduction to the staggering scale of his depravity came with Epstein victim Virginia Roberts Giuffre's January 2015 affidavit, in which she accused Epstein of trafficking her to Britain's Prince Andrew. Page by shocking page, I was stunned by the dark accusations against the royal and other famous men—and certain that sharing them with the world would help support the victims' fight for justice. With photos, flight records, and other documents uncovered, I was sure that these stories would be impossible to ignore.

But my stories—like the women's lawsuits and the reporting of so many others—failed to make much of an impact, or to spark real change at that time. I was frustrated that so many people, like weary parents to a child, seemed to insist, "There's nothing to see here." I was relieved when Epstein was finally arrested in summer 2019, and grateful that his victims would begin to find some sense of closure through his trial and likely conviction.

Of course, we all know how that turned out.

When Epstein died (by suicide or whatever else you may believe), his victims told me that they were disappointed that he'd been able to avoid true justice yet again. He would never pay for the things he had done. Still, so many others remained. In the hours after Epstein's death was announced, Attorney General Bill Barr warned, "co-conspirators should not rest easy." At the same time, the system that employed, enabled, and emboldened them was probably more powerful than ever.

International sex trafficking, drug smuggling, rape, blackmail, political corruption—these are hardly the purview of just one super-villain. Sadly, just as the exploitation of women did not begin with Jeffrey Epstein, so too will it not end with him.

Luckily, though, it has become clear that the fight to expose those monsters of the darkness won't end with him, either.

Harvey Weinstein has been sentenced to 23 years in prison. Other titans and tycoons have been tarnished. Someday soon, the next one will fall. In the meantime, they are watching and waiting, terrified—I'd like to think—that they're next. It probably won't be whom you expect.

***

Just over six months after Epstein's mysterious death in a Manhattan jail cell—and only two months after I released my book *Epstein: Dead Men Tell No Tales*—it was déjà vu all over again as headlines about FBI raids, sex-trafficking rings, and a perverted billionaire splashed across the internet. The FBI had raided a Manhattan office building and retail store belonging to eccentric fashion designer Peter Nygard as part of a sex-trafficking investigation.

Only weeks before that, ten anonymous Jane Does had filed a lawsuit against the Finnish Canadian, alleging that they had been raped, sex trafficked, and otherwise abused over the course of many years. Several of them claimed to have been minors at the time he exploited them. They all claimed that what he did to them was brutal beyond imagination.

Nearly one hundred pages in length, their lawsuit was a disturbing and explosive bombshell. But it was only one drop in an ocean of similar complaints against the so-called "polyester phenom" over the years. Looking back through decades of court documents and long-buried newspaper reports, a history of similar allegations against Nygard comes to the fore. When I traveled to his home in the Bahamas, the aura of evil around his debaucherous estate there was common knowledge—from taxi drivers to house cleaners and politicians alike.

After a few days, I could feel its chill seeping in. One source told me not to go outside after nightfall. Another evening, I got a series of phone calls to my hotel room around the witching hour. The ringer blared persistently at 12:01, 12:34, 1:17. Each time I picked it up, there was no one on the other line. The front desk claimed they didn't know where the calls were coming from. Was it a tech bug or a coded message? Either way, I switched hotel rooms. Incidentally, this was before I learned that the hotel I was staying in had been a sort of staging area for Nygard's female guests before they were picked up and brought out to his exclusive resort. I could picture them standing out front or in the grand lobby, wearing their shortest dresses and highest heels, with no idea what fate awaited them.

Reporting on this case was a full-body experience. Before the FBI raid, I had never even heard of Peter Nygard. (Although his clothes are apparently a hit at Dillard's, I grew up in Massachusetts, more than 565 miles away from the nearest Dillard's store.) Just a few days of immersing myself in his orbit, though, was enough to raise the hairs on the back of my neck. The stink of power, money, corruption, and depravity was familiar to me, but in the Bahamas it was truly redolent.

Digging back into his past through archived newspaper articles and long-buried court documents only exposed more and more layers of rot. Jeffrey Epstein's first recorded sexual assault allegation was in 1997, and he first went to prison for solicitation of a minor a little more than ten years later. Peter Nygard was arrested for rape in 1980. That case vanished into the ether after the victim declined to testify in court, and at press time—more than forty years later—Nygard had never been arrested for a similar offense.

Nygard has always prided himself on being larger than life. Appropriately, the trail of outrageous court claims, massive PR disasters, and legal tussles that he's left in his wake over nearly eighty years is truly breathtaking—and not in a good way.

Despite apparent similarities with men like Jeffrey Epstein and Harvey Weinstein, Peter Nygard is his own kind of animal. A predator with particular appetites, he built his own perverted ecosystem to sate them. For that reason, understanding his life and the allegations against him is a project in and of itself. Once the shock and heartbreak of the stories surrounding him dissipates, one word looms large: HOW?

- How did a farmer's son from Finland grow to become an extravagant icon of the mid-market fashion world?
- How did a department store fashion designer continue to build a multimillion-dollar company even as dozens of horrifying claims of abuse, sexual assault, and harassment were lobbied against him?
- How did he keep his despicable behavior a secret for decades?
- And how many other men like him are hiding in the shadows, wondering when it will be their turn to see their darkest secrets and most shocking crimes exposed?

This is for certain: I'll keep looking for them, finding them, and exposing them, one by one.

—Melissa Cronin

INTRODUCTION

Just before 7 p.m. each day, the Caribbean sun sets over Nassau, the capital of the Bahamas. Vibrant carnival colors streak through the sky, soaring above the hot pink, lime green, and turquoise colonial buildings below. Departing cruise ships pipe party music across the bay: "Can't Stop the Feeling" by Justin Timberlake was the soundtrack for a recent night as vendors packed up their handmade wares at the local straw market, and visiting tourists prepped for another night of fruity cocktails and fried conch.

But passing through the city's outskirts, it gets darker and the lighthearted party mood dissipates. Winding westward through the turns and roundabouts of the island's main thoroughfare—John F. Kennedy Boulevard—the brightly painted buildings of the city give way to crumbling concrete homes overtaken by weeds and vines. Tumbledown liquor stores and hair salons give way to the beat-down scrub at the side of the road. It seems to scroll by endlessly.

Suddenly, the road is blocked by a prim white-trimmed gatehouse. After a few cursory questions, the uniformed guard waves you through, and you enter another world. Stately plantation-style homes loom above impeccably maintained lawns. A vibrant green golf course unfurls on your left, across from the grand salmon-colored clubhouse of the elite Lyford Cay country club—a "1000-acre enclave" that is a "private haven for an international membership," the club's website boasts. Even the local police are not allowed to enter without an invitation.

Still following the winding road, shadows descend. The road narrows, suddenly bordered by impassive stone walls. Foliage hangs heavy overhead. The road follows lazy twists and turns before it dead-ends at the final destination of that forty-minute journey from the heart of Nassau: the massive gate of Nygard Cay, the Caribbean estate of fashion designer Peter Nygard.

Here, the sunset continues over the placid turquoise sea. But inside the property—which is bordered by a barbed-wire fence—the mood is anything but peaceful. Massive cauldrons come to life, blazing with flames. The eyes of concrete Mayan-style gargoyles and snakes across the property glow like embers, smoking with the fire inside. From somewhere inside the labyrinthine property comes an explosion of sound breaking the easy Caribbean nightfall. Angry organ chords in a minor key shoot out across the ocean, the beach, and the surrounding properties: the foreboding first notes of the theme to Andrew Lloyd Webber's *Phantom of the Opera*.

When Peter Nygard was in residence at Nygard Cay, neighbors say, that was the nightly soundtrack. According to scores of young local women, it was indeed the theme song of a real-life monster—one who preyed on women, drugging and raping them at boozy bacchanals on the property. There, celebrities, politicians, and businessmen were treated to decadent, debaucherous experiences that they couldn't find on the mainland. Meanwhile, the young women brought in to fill the female guest list say that like disposable party favors, they were used, abused, and discarded at the night's end. The stories they tell are ones of shame, fear, violation, and blood.

Today, Nygard Cay is abandoned, its owner effectively banned from the Bahamas due to several warrants out for his arrest. Never-ending legal battles with his neighbors, environmental groups, and other foes have left Nygard with few friends and fading power on the island. It's debatable whether he will ever return.

Meanwhile, the paint on his grand Mayan structures is fading, too. Concrete bar stools and gaudy firepits by the water's edge are being overtaken by the sand and sea. Like a haunted house, the property is receding into its surroundings and into history—but the ghosts of what happened there remain, haunting the women who were cursed to cross its doorstep.

This is their story.

CHAPTER 1
BIRTH OF A MONSTER

You don't know how far you can go until you push the limits
—Peter Nygard

Peter Nygard's twisted tale of rape allegations, drugs, and corruption in the Caribbean has a very unlikely beginning: the frozen tundras of Finland. It was there that farmers Hilkka and Eeli Nygard welcomed a son, Peter, on July 24, 1941.

(Over the years, Nygard has sometimes claimed his year of birth was actually 1943—only one of many embellishments perpetuated by the fashion fabulist.)

Looking back on his formative years, Nygard has spun a folksy rags-to-riches tale more captivating than any Hollywood scribe could imagine. Nygard claims that his original family home was a hardscrabble place, "about as far north as anyone can survive." He's said, "I snow-skied before I could walk! We went to school on skis."

Despite the Nygard family's apparent isolation, though, the long fingers of World War II would not spare them as it brought the icy touch of death, hunger, and destruction to Finland and the rest of Europe.

The war-torn 1940s were quite possibly the worst decade to be born as a European, and especially as a Finn. The Soviets had invaded the Scandinavian nation in 1940, and from 1941 to 1945, the Finns joined up with the Nazis to try to get them out. By late 1944 and 1945, however, the Nazis turned against the Finns, in an attempt to seize their nickel mines. That sparked the Lapland War in the northernmost area of Finland—where Nygard claims his family kept their farm.

The Nazis destroyed much of northern Finland throughout that conflict, leaving more than 100,000 people homeless, 1,000 Finnish troops dead, and the Finnish economy decimated. It was in that atmosphere of gunfire and blood that Nygard spent his earliest years.

"He and I were born in the midst of a war," his sister, Pirjo-Liisa Nygard Johnson once explained. "He and I grew up close together all through those war years, on our grandparents' farm."

Even as a child, Nygard pushed boundaries and broke the rules in pursuit of his own pleasure.

"What I remember most of my life with Peter, he cut all my blonde hair off," Liisa, who died in January 2020, once said. "They were shearing sheep at the farm and he figured he would try it on me. . . . all kinds of mischief, but always together."

Shortly after the war ended in 1947, the Nygard family gave up farm life for urban living in Helsinki. Eeli and Hilkka had a bakery, and Peter and Liisa went from playing in the dirt to suiting up for school.

Still, Europe's recovery from the war was a slow one, and more challenges loomed. Nygard's parents feared that the neighboring USSR would eventually invade and seize their fledgling business. So, by 1952 the Nygards were on the move: this time to the tiny town of Deloraine, Manitoba, where they sought political asylum.

According to Nygard lore, Peter's father chose Deloraine because it was just a centimeter away on the map from where his brother lived in Hibbing, Minnesota. Of course, that turned out to be more than an eight-hour drive across an international border.

In any case, Canada still offered a chance for a better life than the one the Nygards had built in Finland. In the beginning, though, they may have felt some regrets.

"I started in the most humble beginnings," Nygard has said. For once, that seems to be an understatement.

The four Nygards made their home in a converted coal shed that was roughly eighty square feet inside. Photos of the structure remain, and it appears to be every bit as bare-bones as it sounds.

"We didn't have any water, we didn't have any electricity," Nygard has said. "We were literally at the bottom of the barrel, you know?" An ancient stove was the only source of heat inside, and the family's bathroom was an outhouse two hundred yards away from the main structure, where temperatures could reach forty degrees below zero in the winter.

"Somehow we crawled out of it," Nygard admitted in an interview. In later years, that home would be preserved at the Nygard International headquarters in Winnipeg—a reminder of how far Nygard had come.

By 1967, the family had moved to the capital city of Winnipeg, and Nygard's father secured a position at a bank. Later, his parents would own and operate their own bakery, just as they had done in Finland.

Things were looking up for the Nygards, and young Peter began to stretch his wings as a budding businessman.

Nygard once told a reporter that one of his earliest hobbies was "collecting Coke bottles from ditches . . . and selling them for 2 cents a piece so we could buy water, which was 25 cents, and survive another day." By age twelve, he had started his own paper route, and was even able to buy a bike with the profits.

At the same time, he was starting to nurture his competitive side through sports. According to old yearbook photos, Nygard attended Norberry Junior High in Winnipeg, where he was a member of the basketball team.

Another former student of Norberry says that the school was a rough place to come of age.

"The methods of discipline may have been more strict than nowadays, but we all survived," Norberry grad John Hindle wrote in the *Winnipeg Free Press*.

"One time a phys-ed teacher threw a volleyball halfway across the gym, hitting a kid who was fooling around to get his attention. It was quite a throw."

On another occasion, Hindle remembered, "I handed in an essay in Grade 9 that was four pages, hand-written and double-spaced. When it was returned, the teacher had written a critique in red ink in every available space on the paper, including sideways across the top and bottom of the page, just for emphasis."

At the same time, Nygard and the other students at Norberry were spending their preteen years in the shadow of the cold war. Even in Canada, the students were forced to do nuclear air raid drills, hiding under their desks in the classroom until they got the all clear. It was a time when opportunity and evil seemed to linger in the air.

After Norberry, Nygard continued on to the nearby Glenlawn Collegiate high school. Working as a lifeguard, his income grew and he was able to buy his first car. Before long though, he has claimed, he sold it to help his parents open a bakery of their own.

With his parents secure and high school behind him, Nygard was ready to leave his small town in the dust. He crossed the border to America for college.

"My cousins, who lived in Hibbing, Minnesota, invited me to come to the junior college there, which I attended for about a year," he told *UND Today* in 2019. "One day, as I was driving back to Winnipeg, I drove through Grand Forks and through the campus of UND (University of North Dakota), and I fell in love with it. So the following year, I decided that it was the university for me."

"Attending UND was something I had dreamed about when I was in Winnipeg," he said. "I never realized how phenomenal college life could really be. I was in awe of UND."

Nygard definitely took advantage of the opportunity. Instead of spending his time on the basketball court like in high school, he joined the campus business fraternity, Delta Sigma Pi, and later became president. He claims he was even recognized nationally for how well he ran the organization. Strangely, in all of his stories about college life, there's little talk about girls. Nygard's version of the story is that he was a monk-like mogul in the making as he prepared to take the business world by storm.

"The most important lesson I learned at UND was realizing my future life was not going to be only about sports," he told *UND Today.* "Instead, I focused on and prepared myself for the business world. Somehow at UND, I developed a vision of my future, and I prepared myself for my next stage in life. I learned to study, focus, and be committed."

"My favorite classes were all that pertained to business, including economics, business law, and marketing. I found the business curriculum to be outstanding, and I excelled in it. The amount of information I was absorbing was challenging to me, and the further I went in the school, the better I got in class," he claimed. "I eventually became almost a straight-A student in my last year." He graduated in 1964 with a degree in business.

Riding high on his college success (and more than a little bit of ego), Nygard quickly landed a job with Eaton's, Canada's largest department store chain at the time. Nygard has claimed that an entry-level position was not in the cards for someone like him. According to Nygard lore, he took an aptitude test that identified him as a prime candidate to take over as the president of the company. Instead, he started as little more than an errand boy, sweeping floors, stocking shelves, and even hauling bags of manure. He says he made the decision himself so that he could learn the business from the ground up.

"I was never afraid to get my hands dirty," Nygard told the University of North Dakota *Alumni Review* in 2019. Still, he was chasing the smell of success—and it wasn't manure.

Nygard quickly rose to an executive position at Eaton's, where he oversaw more than $250 million in sales across the continent. Yet that quickly proved to be an insufficient challenge.

In 1967, Nygard quit his position at Eaton's and took a pay cut to work for a fashion designer at a struggling clothing line, Nathan Jacob's Tan Jay. Nygard saw it more as an opportunity than as a dream position. He later explained, "I ended up tumbling into the fashion industry accidentally!"

Even though the brand was not yet profitable, Nygard borrowed $8,000 so he could take Jacob up on his offer to buy 20 percent of the business.

Within three years, Nygard owned the entire company, which he soon christened Nygard.

From the start, Nygard was a risk-taker. These are just some of the many
innovations he claims as his own:

- The first North American clothing line to expand into Asia
- The first Canadian business to use air-conditioned factories
- The fastest distribution system the world had ever seen
- Overall, the "number one company in the world in technology"
  by the 1990s

"We took what Henry Ford did with cars by creating a system to move prod-
uct fast and meet the demand," he said in the late 1990s. "It's the fastest
system. No one else has the capacity to do this."

By the end of 1998, he claimed, his company was so tech-savvy that they
didn't even use paper. "If you send us paper," he said at the time, "we have a
conversion center to convert that paper into electronics and send you a bill."

The results spoke for themselves. Nygard was able to grow the company
quickly, spinning out a variety of lines over the years: Peter Nygard, Nygard
Collection, Tan Jay, Nygard Slims, Bianca Nygard, Westbound, Investments,
Allison Daley, ALIA, and more. Together, the lines targeted women thirty-
five years old and up, largely in the mid-price range. Forbes crowned him a
"polyester phenom" in 2010, when his net worth was said to be nearly $900
million.

At its peak, the Nygard empire had more than 170 dedicated stores in
North America, plus 6,000 "shop-in-shops" at department stores. Nygard
boasted one million square feet of distribution space across the continent,
shipping more than twenty million pieces of clothing each year for total rev-
enues supposedly topping $1 billion. For that reason, he thought of himself
as the founder of "fast fashion."

As a group, Nygard's companies had more than fifteen thousand employees, and offices in New York, L.A., Toronto, Winnipeg, Shanghai, and more.

In the futuristic New York flagship, customers could watch fashion shows in the "iLounge" as chrome mannequins rotated nearby. Nygard's name was spelled out in giant neon letters at least four times across the face of the building.

By the early 2000s, he was on top of the world, and he was happy to tell anyone who would listen. "Sometimes I feel like Mick Jagger," he once said, bragging, "You know, I invented the casual Friday look: jeans, cowboy boots and a jacket." His hometown of Deloraine, Manitoba, even opened "Nygard Park," featuring a plaque with his grinning face.

His colleagues were just as happy to sing his praises.

"He's been a great partner," Alex Dillard, president of the Dillard's chain, said once in a video tribute. "He's changed the way I think about the retail business." (That was of course before he canceled orders with Nygard in light of the sex-trafficking investigation.)

By all accounts, this period of Nygard's life truly appeared to be the epitome of a rags-to-riches tale. Pulling himself up by his ski straps, athletic, charming, and blond Peter Nygard was essentially a living folk hero for his fellow Canadians. He had crawled his way up from the tundra to the heights of glamor, profit, and fame.

It was a great story. But it wasn't the whole story. Behind the scenes, another Peter Nygard was taking form: someone who was accused of being a ruthless predator who would ruin the lives of countless women—before he destroyed his own.

CHAPTER 2
FILTHY RICH

He literally ruined my life.
—Fashion designer Nancy Ebker

In 1975, young designer Nancy Ebker was the toast of the fashion elite in New York City. The July "Fashion Talk" column in the *New York Times* raved about the "graceful" culotte skirts she had crafted for the Jonathan Logan corporation (then the country's largest women's apparel company). *Times* reporter Bernardine Morris wrote that the culottes were "a fashion that is much more widely accepted in Europe than it is in this country," but one that "should gain in popularity as a result of Miss Ebker's knowledgeable treatment."

Ebker was a tastemaker for America's most stylish fashionistas. Indeed, her 1975 designs made such a splash that the very next year, she was recruited to be president of the Susan Thomas Sportswear Division, a conglomerate encompassing several clothing lines. The labels were not doing well, but Ebker was up for the challenge. She was a trailblazer, the only American woman serving as president of a major fashion company at the time. As such, she was compensated handsomely, with a salary of up to $187,500 per year, or nearly $1,000,000 in 2020 dollars.

Ebker worked quickly to turn the businesses around, but a year later the Susan Thomas parent company, Genesco, announced they were getting out of apparel to focus on footwear and accessories. Ebker was stunned and more than a little upset. Before closing up shop, however, Genesco offered to let her buy the lines and continue them on the strength of her reputation alone.

Ebker would need about $1,000,000 to make it work—a sum of money she did not have. Friends at other corporations turned down her pleas for investment, and she began to entertain draconian deals. It was looking hopeless. Then, she heard from Peter Nygard.

At a meeting in Ebker's Manhattan offices, Nygard offered to cut a deal that seemed almost too good to be true. He would allow Ebker to continue running two of her lines, Sportswork-Nancy Ebker, and Vivo. He even assured her that he would be hands-off, strictly "absentee management."

Ebker cobbled together a complicated deal with Nygard over several days. Then, when it came time to put it into writing, Nygard balked. Ever the smooth talker, he insisted that a verbal agreement would suffice for the time being. There was some vague talk about Canadian lawyers and international delays. Ebker agreed to take Nygard at his word so she could get to work—a decision she would spend the rest of her life regretting.

It didn't take long before everything fell apart. Soon, Ebker has said, "it became readily apparent that the newly formed partnership was not being operated in the manner in which she had anticipated." That was an understatement.

Nygard "bombarded" Ebker and her staff with rapid-fire memos about how the company would be run. He decided to remove the company's only water cooler for a savings of $30 per month. He sent Ebker a memo advising her and her staff that any purchase they made had to be approved by officers at his company, Tan Jay. He slashed salaries for Ebker's staff, despite allegedly having promised her that he would keep all compensation at its normal level. Ebker even claimed that he moved her office from the front of her spacious showroom to inside a tiny storage room.

Ebker was horrified as Nygard went further and further to take control of the fashion line bearing her name. She sued, and described her reaction to his attempted coup in court:

> I said, "Peter, you can't do this! We're partners."
> He said, "We have nothing in writing and I never intended to put anything in writing."

I said, "You can't do this! This is the United States and we are partners."

He said, "You have nothing; I am a millionaire."

He said, "If you want anything pertaining to Nancy Ebker, you are going to pay me a million dollars since I will no longer have the benefit of using your name."

I said, "Peter, you cannot do this."

I said, "Let's try to reason. . . . I will finish designing my line, we will separate in an equitable way."

He said, "No."

He said, "You will pay me a million dollars by Friday for everything pertaining to [your line] including the patterns, the samples, and the orders Genesco gave you."

And he said, "If you don't have a million dollars by Friday, I am going to see to it that your name and reputation are totally destroyed in this market."

Then he said, "I don't think that should be too difficult considering you are just a woman."

Female executives were rare at the time, and not just in fashion. Nygard's words and behavior must have cut Ebker deep. Of course, his version of events was totally different. Nygard insisted in court that Ebker's testimony was little more than an emotional breakdown, and he was prepared to share the cold, hard facts. He told the court:

I said in effect that I did not feel the arrangements under which we were working was working to either one of our satisfaction, and that I wished to terminate this arrangement and really not go on with the company.

I wanted to do it amicably and I wanted to give her every opportunity to find other arrangements or other financiers . . .

I offered to her any way I can to have a smooth transition, and I

suggested and highly recommended that we keep this very amica-
ble and do it as smoothly as we can so it would not hurt either one
of us.

I recalled her staying quite calm and silent.

Judge Irving Cooper wasn't buying it. After both designers had their say,
Cooper released a ruling that chastised Nygard but offered little relief for his
female adversary. He wrote:

> We were favorably impressed by the straightforward testimony of
> Ebker, and found her to be a sincere and candid witness. She
> impressed us with her veracity and consistent testimony.
> Furthermore, [Nygard's] repeated attempts to impeach the credi-
> bility of Ebker only served to reinforce our conviction that Ebker
> was a highly credible witness . . .
>
> Nygard's demeanor on the witness stand was evasive and insin-
> cere, and he contradicted himself on numerous occasions through-
> out the course of his testimony . . .
>
> We unhesitatingly find the testimony of Nygard utterly lacking
> in credibility, and we reject his testimony insofar as it contradicts
> that of plaintiff.

Nevertheless, it was the Finnish fashion designer who ultimately could claim
victory. The judge wrote:

> Despite the fact that we deplore the unseemly conduct of Nygard,
> both during the lifetime of the joint venture, and in the winding
> up period, we nevertheless find that plaintiff has failed to persuade
> us by a fair preponderance of the credible evidence that she was
> damaged by the actions of Nygard.
>
> Moreover, although plaintiff alleges that she brought valuable
> assets to the partnership, she has failed to provide us with any

legal authority in support of her position that the assets which she contributed to the joint venture should be considered in an accounting. Furthermore, although plaintiff has established that Nygard acted in bad faith in the manner in which he wound down the partnership, plaintiff has not in any respects established that she was damaged as a result of such conduct.

In short, the judge seemed to suggest that she brought nothing to their partnership, and therefore could not have been damaged by its implosion. Ebker's claims were dismissed, as were the counterclaims that Nygard had brought against her. They were each ordered to pay their own legal fees.

Would the judge have reached the same conclusion if Ebker were a man? Either way, she never would regain her status as a leading American designer. Ebker later told *Forbes* that Nygard had "ruined" her life. She said, he was "a true villain of the world."

She would not be the last woman to feel that way.

***

As the Ebker case wound its way through the courts in New York, there was trouble brewing back home for Nygard in Winnipeg.

The news broke quietly, as a roughly seventy-five-word paragraph appeared on the wires in Canada on January 18, 1980. Tucked into crime roundups of the local papers, it didn't even merit a front-page placement. But despite the lack of fanfare, the headline was shocking: Dashing young fashion mogul Peter Nygard had been accused of rape.

According to the report, Nygard had been arrested on January 16, 1980, after an eighteen-year-old woman told Winnipeg police that he had raped her. In court, Nygard paid a $7,500 bond to walk free until trial. The judge ordered that no details of the hearing could be made public by the media. There was little else for reporters to say.

The case remained out of the papers for weeks until another headline came across the wires in June: "Rape Charge Stayed in Peter Nygard Case."

According to the *Winnipeg Free Press*, when Nygard's teen accuser took the stand, she had declined to testify.

"We put her on the stand and asked the appropriate questions," the prosecutor told the paper, "but she didn't want to say anything."

The case was stayed—an extremely rare occurrence in Canadian courts, and one that left Nygard with no criminal offenses on his record. The alleged victim would never speak publicly again.

Nygard, of course, had plenty to say. Not long after the charge was dropped, he blasted police for using "poor judgment" in going after the case. According to the *Winnipeg Free Press*, he said, "that the whole matter could have been avoided had they adopted a more sensible attitude."

In addition, the paper noted, Nygard proclaimed he was planning to start a watchdog foundation "that will finance the work needed to improve the quality of the justice system."

Later that year, he hinted to the *Brandon Sun* newspaper that several famous names had already committed to his cause. He declined to reveal them, and it appears that the foundation never went anywhere—just like the charges.

As the rape case faded into the background, Nygard had no trouble finding female companions. Like Ebker, though, many of them would later regret ever meeting him, and would spend years of their lives in court fighting to make him pay.

Nygard's parade of partners began when he married blonde Winnipeg model and socialite Carolyn Knight on September 20, 1968. The local paper gushed over their picture-perfect wedding, describing the bride's "triple-tiered crown of iridescent crystals" and the gowns of every member of the bridal party. Less than two years later, however, the bright young couple were separated, and Nygard moved on to another blonde.

This time, he met flight attendant Patricia Bickle when she was on a layover in Waikiki, and he was on his way back from business dealings in Asia. Nygard moved fast.

"He asked me specifically to get pregnant, and begged me to take my IUD out," Bickle later said. She obliged before they even walked down the aisle. Bickle would give birth to a daughter, Bianca, in 1977, another daughter, Alia, in 1979, and later, a son, Kai. But in the years before the children were born, Nygard was hedging his bets and continuing his bed-hopping.

In 1973, while in the midst of hooking up with Bickle, Nygard met brunette model Helena Jaworski in Winnipeg. Within a few months, she was pregnant, too. Their child, Peter, was born on April 21, 1974.

From the start, Jaworski has claimed, Nygard was a distant dad. "There were no monthly payments, but he would give Peter gifts or money and make promises," she told *Toronto Life* in 2006. "And because he was my son's father, I assumed he would come through."

She assumed wrong.

Nygard refused to play a major role in the life of his namesake son, she said, so Jaworski began child-support proceedings in 1976. At the time, Canadian courts did not consider income when awarding child support, and Jaworski received a judgment of just $150 per month. She kept fighting, and in 1977—the year Nygard's next child, Bianca, was born to Bickle—she was awarded $1,500 per month.

Still, Nygard failed to pay yet again, and Jaworski went to court for the next decade to try to force the millionaire to support their child. A judge in the case later wrote, "It is really quite pathetic to read what this mother has had to do and give up in order to give [her son] a reasonable standard of living. She has sold almost everything she has in an effort to assist the child."

Meanwhile, Bickle had been living out of sight, out of mind, in the Bahamas while Nygard's messy court case with Jaworski raged on in Canada. By 1986, though, it seems he tired of having Bickle and the brood hanging around his party paradise. According to reports, Nygard strongly suggested that she pack up their kids and move to Switzerland, even offering to buy her an apartment there. They settled on shared custody with a child-support stipend of $7,000 per month, and Nygard was freed up to move on to his next conquest.

That same year, in 1986, Nygard started dating another blonde flight attendant, Kaarina Pakka. Pakka was a Finn too, and she has said that a smitten Nygard told her he wanted her to give him a fully Finnish heir. When she did indeed become pregnant, Pakka once told *Toronto Life*, "He wasn't *un*happy about it." From the start, however, it became clear that she too would have to fight him to support their child.

Pakka told *Toronto Life* that Nygard didn't show up for the child's birth, as he had promised. Instead, he sent flowers and a toy to her home. Pakka "was beginning to realize she had been naive to trust Nygard," the magazine claimed. "She and Nygard spoke on the phone occasionally, but his attention was as inconsistent as his support payments."

At one point, she told the magazine, she received a random envelope with $300 in it, which she considered "an insult."

According to the magazine, Pakka "claimed Nygard told her he had fathered three other children and he never paid support." When it became apparent that that would be his attitude toward their son, Mika, too, she began child-support proceedings in 1988.

Pakka told *Toronto Life* that Nygard was livid over her decision, and warned her that proceeding down the legal route would effectively end his relationship with her and Mika. She even claimed that Nygard said a court battle would mean he'd come to think of their son as little more than "an expensive fuck." Already, though, it was clear to Pakka that Nygard would never be the kind of father she'd envisioned. She claimed he'd only seen their son twice in the first three and a half years of his life.

Disillusioned with Nygard's behavior so far, Pakka pressed forward. She would spend the next fifteen years battling it out with the billionaire in court.

By 2000, Nygard was pulling in more than $300 million in yearly revenues, but still not supporting Pakka to the extent she felt she deserved. So, she hired a cutthroat attorney who demanded that she be awarded $68,000 per month, plus $5.5 million in retroactive payments. If granted, it would be the largest child-support payment ever ordered in the history of Canada at the time, but her attorney broke down a budget showing how the amount was really quite logical in their minds. That budget included $38,000 per year in vacation expenses, and more than $900 per month for "entertainment." The Canadian media was skeptical, to say the least.

The case finally reached a confidential settlement in 2004—an outcome Pakka's attorney said she was "very happy" with. For his part, Nygard hired a lobbyist and launched a crusade against the country's divorce laws and their supposed discrimination against men. Like so many of his revenge projects, this one seemed to peter out over time.

Publicly, though, he insisted the whole debacle was much ado about nothing. "Mr. Nygard has always taken care of his children," a rep told the *Globe and Mail* Canada at the time. The rep even shared a quote from Nygard's daughter with Patricia Bickle, Bianca, then 17. "Our dad has always taken care of all us kids including Mika," she said, "financially and otherwise."

(Bianca, in particular, had always been one of Nygard's favorites. The year before she distributed that statement, he had hosted her Sweet Sixteen at Nygard Cay. Nygard was so proud, he commemorated the event by releasing a VHS tape of the party to the public. On the back of the videocassette sleeve was a dedication he had written to her: "I want to be the first man you remember. I want to be the last man you forget.")

In the end, Pakka said that the entire experience had taught her something disturbing about Peter Nygard. It didn't have anything to do with money, or family, or his willingness to take on a legal fight. She later told *Toronto Life* that he thinks of sex "as a release mechanism. It's how he deals with the pressures of business. It's like going out and running or doing push-ups or whatever people do."

The only difference? His method of stress release had the potential to destroy women's lives. The world would soon find out about it.

CHAPTER 3
HU$H MONEY

*If you ask women who work for me, they'd say I'm the biggest pro-
moter of women and female causes that they've ever met.*
—Peter Nygard

Nygard's rape arrest did not seem to chasten him. If anything, the ease with
which it all blew over appears to have emboldened him. Multiple employees
have claimed that in the years after his arrest, he was an unrestrained sexual predator who made his offices his hunting ground and his employees
his prey.

Their stories shared chilling similarities across the board, and had disturbing details that were each woman's alone.

One, a thirty-two-year-old single mother, was hired as a merchandiser at
Nygard International in the years after Nygard's rape case was dismissed.
She had heard the rumors about his behavior, she told *Toronto Life* in 2006,
but steeled herself to push through any impropriety. She had no idea what
she was in for.

Just a few months after the woman started work, Nygard sent her to
Hong Kong to meet with some of his manufacturers.

"When she arrived she was ushered into a VIP suite at a hotel, where she
noticed a door to an adjoining suite that had no handle on her side," *Toronto
Life* described. "She asked the manager about it, and he told her the other
side wasn't rented."

"In the middle of the night, she claims, she awoke to find Nygard, bare-chested, standing over her. She started to cry. He told her everything would be fine, no one else had to know."

The woman, Jonna Laursen, later told the *New York Times* that he had raped her.

The trip only became more nightmarish from there, in Laursen's accounting. Speaking anonymously back in 2006, she told *Toronto Life* that although it was not in her job description, Nygard forced her to model sample clothing in meetings with their Asian colleagues—and he didn't exactly keep it professional.

"One time he jumped forward and grabbed my left breast, asking if it was padded," she told the magazine, "as it looked bigger than the right one."

Nygard's colleagues seemed to love it, she said, but for her it was the pinnacle of humiliation and sexual degradation.

The woman stuck it out for two years, debating whether or not she should go. Ultimately, Nygard made the decision for her and she was fired. Furious, she exploded in her final HR meeting, threatening to go to the papers and expose what she had endured as Nygard's right-hand woman. She stormed out of the office, her head spinning with the indignity of it all.

Only a few hours later, she said, a company executive showed up at her door with a check for $8,000 and a legal document for her to sign. She took it. Her experience with Nygard would stay secret for decades.

Before she left, though, Laursen shared her story with another colleague, Dale Dreffs. Dreffs was no stranger to Nygard's predatory behavior. In fact, she claimed, there was hardly any woman at the company who *hadn't* heard about it.

"Everyone was fearful," Dreffs told *Toronto Life*. Indeed, in those years it seemed that everyone—if they were female—had a story.

Dreffs had a few. On one occasion, she claimed, Nygard called her into his office suite and "spoke to her while sitting on the toilet with his pants down."

At another meeting, this time with colleagues, Nygard allegedly pushed the boundaries even further. *Toronto Life* reported, "He asked her to stand beside him at his desk. A few of his executives were seated at the other side of it. He started to run his foot up and down her thigh." She quit after just six months.

Another employee, Debra McDonald, claimed to have had a totally different but equally disturbing experience. In 2020, she told the *New York Times* that she joined the Nygard operation in 1978—two years *before* Nygard would be arrested for rape. McDonald claims the harassment began immediately.

Nygard constantly attempted to grab her breasts, she told the paper, an accusation that other former employees have lobbed as well.

In one particularly horrifying incident, she claimed, Nygard called her in to a meeting. What did she find behind his office door? It wasn't him sitting on a toilet or masturbating, as other women claim to have witnessed. During McDonald's meeting, she said, Nygard greeted her while graphic pornography played in the background. "I was so disgusted," she told the *Times*. She finally quit not long after Nygard's rape arrest in 1980.

That arrest, it seems, did little to slow him down. Nearly fifteen years later, in 1995, the *New York Times* reported that a former employee sued Nygard for having sex with her "against her will" in his Winnipeg office. According to the newspaper report, her attorney has said that the suit resulted in a nondisclosure agreement.

(By the "Me Too" era, nondisclosure agreements would become known as a tool of sexual predators—one used to keep their victims silent and under their control. Lawmakers in New York, New Jersey, and Pennsylvania recently introduced bills to make NDAs illegal in cases of sexual harassment. Nygard, it seems, was an early adapter.)

Predation. Humiliation. Debasement. Shame. Across the decades, female Nygard Company employees were sharing the stories of what their boss was allegedly doing behind closed doors. Meanwhile, in public, he couldn't stop talking about how he was such a friend to the entire gender.

"In my opinion, a woman is every bit as good of a leader as a man," he once opined. "And in fact, perhaps even better. In many ways, I feel that if there were more women leaders in this world, we would not have wars. Women know how to give; men many times only take."

By the mid-nineties, it was becoming apparent that the leader of one of Canada's biggest corporations felt justified in doing and taking whatever he wanted.

***

One June 22, 1996, the front page of the *Winnipeg Free Press* carried a huge glamor shot of a grinning and tuxedoed Peter Nygard. That in itself wasn't unusual; he was certainly a local celebrity—and one fixated on generating his own positive PR. The headline above the photo, though, would have made even the spotlight-seeking fashion mogul wince: "Ex-staff Claim Verbal Abuse, Humiliation, Harassment"

Across several pages, the paper laid out a damning narrative, the result of extensive interviews "with seven former and current female employees" at Nygard's company—three of whom recently had filed sexual-harassment claims against him. These employees shared what they had endured while working for Nygard in Toronto, Winnipeg, Los Angeles, and the Bahamas. The picture that they painted of their boss was more than disturbing. Readers used to photos of Nygard at galas, fund-raisers, and fashion shows must have been stunned.

According to these women, Nygard was far from a jocular millionaire playboy. Instead, they claimed, he was secretly "domineering," volatile, abusive, and "had no regard for women."

Nygard often would "scream and swear at employees for hours," the women alleged, "berating them over their work and humiliating them in front of co-workers." Even worse, more than one alleged that he had sexually assaulted them. Others claimed that they had witnessed his sexual advances toward colleagues.

The accounts of the three women who filed sexual-harassment complaints—with the Manitoba Human Rights Commission—were chilling in their similarity. According to the paper, Nygard had paid out $20,000 in settlements in that year alone over sex assault claims. (That's more than $300,000 in 2020 dollars.)

The records from the Human Rights Commission are not public, so there is no official record of what they told the authorities. In the paper, however, Allison Adams, Judy Shier, and a woman simply referred to as "Mary Ann" all laid bare the horror of their experiences working for Peter Nygard. This is what they had to say.

JUDY

"I'm not naive," Judy Shier told the *Winnipeg Free Press.* "I'm pretty much known as a kick-ass broad. But I have never in my life seen something like this."

Serving as Nygard's communications manager, Shier was by his side constantly, both in the office and around the world. She was privy to some of his most private moments—and what she saw disgusted her.

"Every time we went into his office to get something, his pants were open and his hands were down his pants," Shier claimed. Those assaults weren't even the half of it, she said. According to the paper, she told the Manitoba Human Rights Commission of five different incidents where he had subjected her to sexual harassment.

On the road with her boss, the harassment seemed even more inescapable. Shier continued, "The Bahamas made me decide this was just no life. It was there that I had seen he had no regard for women. You'd go into his office and he'd be in his red Speedo bathing suit with his hands down his pants. He was always making remarks about my breasts."

"So I went to L.A.," she said, "and it was even worse. His office was in his bedroom. You have to go up there and he's half-dressed, and he's fondling himself."

Shier claimed to have put up with a lot over the years, but there were some things that she felt were beyond the pale. The final straw in her own personal nightmare came one day when she made a disturbing discovery during office work. Shier was told to go fetch an item from the closet in Nygard's office/bedroom suite. She hurried off to complete her task, with no idea of what was to come. Shier opened the closet door, and there laying before her, open for the world to see, was allegedly "a fax paper box filled with pornographic pictures, featuring Nygard and women."

Shier quit, and filed a sexual-harassment claim with the Human Rights Commission. She later would receive a $6,000 payoff from Nygard International.

Before that, though, Shier was responsible for hiring the woman who would become Nygard's next target: a tall young blonde named Allison Adams.

Shier admitted that she had her doubts about bringing another lamb in for the slaughter, so to speak. "It was like I sacrificed a life or something," she told the *Winnipeg Free Press*. "It was just gross."

Her fears were confirmed on Adams's first day, Shier claimed, when Adams's new boss "walked up to her, stroked her behind, and put his hand on her ass."

"He turned to me," Shier described, "and said, 'She is absolutely beautiful.'"

ALLISON

Allison Adams was a recent graduate of Success Business College in Winnipeg when she took a position at Nygard International as a travel coordinator. As Shier described, Nygard allegedly had his eye on her from the beginning.

Only three days into the job, Adams found herself at an evening board meeting that was running late with Nygard and two other female colleagues. As they ordered in pizza to work through dinner, Adams told the group that she'd have to leave before wrapping up. She was booked to sing with her band JFK and the Conspirators at a local dive bar in downtown Winnipeg.

Adams left to perform at the Junkyard at the Portage Village Inn, thinking the incident had barely registered with the man responsible for running her multimillion-dollar employer. She was idly drinking beers with friends, thinking nothing of her earlier comment at work, when her new boss walked in. Adams was overwhelmed seeing one of Canada's richest men—who also happened to be her new boss—in a run-down dive. She told the *Winnipeg Free Press* "she respectfully put out her hand to shake his." But according to Adams, that wasn't what Nygard had in mind.

"He kissed her on both cheeks, fondled her buttocks, and suggested they go to a corner where they could 'neck,'" the paper claimed.

Thinking fast, Adams instead pulled Nygard over to introduce him to her bandmates and her brother. They all struck up a conversation, and she escaped unharmed—that time.

Nygard wasn't used to not getting his way. According to Adams, his sexual advances only intensified after her rejection. After a while, it seemed, he got the hint.

He wasn't happy about it, to say the least. Adams claimed she suffered ongoing verbal abuse from Nygard when it became clear that she would not give in to his advances. She claimed he regularly subjected her to nasty tirades, blasting her as "incompetent" and worse.

Of course, it couldn't last. Adams was fired, and she quickly filed a sexual-harassment complaint with the Human Rights Commission. She received an $8,000 check from Nygard International.

MARY ANN

A "spooked" Mary Ann requested that the *Winnipeg Free Press* only refer to her by her first name as she shared the details of what she experienced during her employment as Nygard's assistant. At the time of her interview, Nygard's shadow still loomed large in Winnipeg and all of Canada.

Her story, like so many others, was one of escalating assaults.

The first sign that something was wrong, she said, was something she tried to explain away. Nygard would "come out in his bathrobe," she claimed, explaining, "That would kind of put me off." Ultimately, she decided that it wasn't something to give up her paycheck over.

Soon, though, her resolve would be tested.

One day Nygard, "called me in to get some work," Mary Ann told the *Winnipeg Free Press*, "and he was stroking himself at his desk. He had his hands inside his pants and I looked at him like he was some kind of pig."

She remembered turning her back on her boss to compose herself—in the hopes that he might take a hint and compose himself as well. When she turned back around, however, Nygard had allegedly done the opposite.

Mary Ann claimed, "He pulled his pants way down and he was stroking himself looking at me." She resigned on February 9, 1996, and filed a sexual-harassment claim with the Manitoba Human Rights Commission. Nygard International gave her a $4,500 check.

DEBORAH

Former Nygard employee Deborah Wagner was one of the women who did not file a sexual-harassment claim against her boss. Although she claimed that Nygard often verbally abused her, it was what she saw happening to others that really chilled her to her core.

Like Mary Ann, Wagner served as Nygard's personal assistant. Instead of Winnipeg, she was assigned to his Marina Del Rey, California, home/office. Among her many duties, she said, was the gargantuan task of organizing "pamper days" that would bring hairdressers, manicurists, and masseuses to the house. At first, they were just for Nygard. They would later become the crux of Nygard's alleged scheme of sexual assault. In the meantime, though, Wagner was responsible for organizing Nygard's evening activities as well.

Nygard's three-story residence featured five bedrooms on the main level, and Wagner said he took full advantage of every one. "I juggled five women in one night," she told the *Winnipeg Free Press*. Beyond the sheer numbers, Wagner said she was disturbed by what she saw. "You cannot believe what goes on in his house, and how he treats women," she told the paper. "It makes you physically sick."

In just one example, Wagner claimed girls were locked in their respective bedrooms so that they couldn't escape and mistakenly stumble into another woman's room. According to Nygard's employees, the doors were fitted with locks on both sides.

***

Wagner was tasked with organizing Nygard's own personal "pamper days," but before long he would turn the practice into a signature event: the pamper party. Nygard's "pamper parties" were gatherings around the globe, where he would treat young women to manicures, massages, and hair appointments in his homes. Usually, there were few men other than Nygard to be found.

The parties began at least as far back as the nineties, and were happening as recently as 2018. A video from that year posted to Instagram takes viewers inside what one Nygard guest called the "world-famous" event.

According to the cameraman, roughly a dozen of Nygard's "really beautiful friends" had been invited to get manicures, eat BBQ ribs, and shake their rear ends at the camera. Nearly all were scantily clad in short shorts, crop tops, and lots of spandex.

"These girls are getting pampered over here," the cameraman boasts in the clip. "This is Nygard's world-famous pamper day. Unbelievable."

The same man—who is definitely well into middle age—also posted a video of a beach volleyball day at the L.A. home's "Nygard Beach." A gaggle of young blonde Instagram models had gathered for the day, as well as YouTuber Jack Payne.

Nygard's L.A. home wasn't the only place where he mixed business with pleasure. In his Winnipeg office, it seemed he didn't even try to hide the extent of his appetites.

From the beginning, it was more party pad than executive office. In a 1978 *Winnipeg Free Press* article that crowned Nygard the "Viking Gatsby," the reporter breathlessly gushed over Nygard's bachelor pad.

"The amazing Mr. Nygard is not content just making piles of money," the author wrote. "He also spends it with an outrageous flamboyance that leaves the casual observer speechless. His private executive office, for example, is a veritable ode to Nygard's curious blend of sensuous hedonism and steely practicality."

"At first glance," he continued, "it seems a typical millionaire playboy's den, designed more for the pursuits of the flesh than any financial carryings-on. Plush carpet, soft lighting, a passion pit complete with a sofa that converts into a bed at the push of a button, and a mirror-equipped ceiling. 'The floor is heated,' he chortles, 'so in the winter you can walk around barefoot or roll around bare if you choose.'"

"The place is festooned with the lush foliage of plants which give the impression that one is in a forest glade rather than a converted farm machinery warehouse," the reporter described.

It is only when "a folding wall rolls away to reveal a complex private command centre" that the business side of the equation presents itself.

Two years later, a different reporter for the *Brandon Sun* newspaper named the office a "passion pit" as well.

"At the push of a button, the sofa transforms into a giant bed," the reporter described. "Press another button and the well-equipped bar in the corner becomes an equally well-equipped kitchen."

"Further on, a concealed door leads to a lavish bedroom," he continued, "complete with a hidden telephone, a shower, and a sauna."

According to the allegations of his employees, that Winnipeg office, his Marina Del Rey home, and so many locations around the world were more than just places for Nygard to get a day's work done. They were international sex dens, where Nygard perpetrated his desires on the women that surrounded him—whether they wanted it or not. It was a web of dark secrets. But none of it would compare to Nygard Cay.

CHAPTER 4
A PERVERT'S PARADISE

I get what I want.
—Peter Nygard

A son of the tundras, Nygard first began to escape from Canada to the Bahamas in the 1970s. "I spent all my life in the snow," he once said. "The novelty of the sun and the Caribbean attracted me when I could afford it."

Beyond the good weather, the Bahamas had a reputation at the time for being flexible with laws—and filled with people who loved to break them. It all began in the early 1960s, when Castro's victory in Cuba inspired organized crime boss Meyer Lansky to move his operations to the nearby islands of the Bahamas. Under Lansky's "suggestion," casino gambling was quickly legalized in the island nation. With that came an influx of international banks that allowed newly flush international businessmen to conduct their financial dealings beneath a cloak of secrecy.

According to Alan A. Block, author of *Masters of Paradise: Organized Crime & the IRS in the Bahamas*, this period of growth sparked pervasive political corruption that has continued in the Bahamas almost to this day.

"Poor countries which live on the proceeds of parasitic industries such as casino gambling, offshore banking, and drug smuggling often seem on the verge of totally submitting to illicit interests," Block wrote. "In the Bahamas, it happened. A process of criminalization that started with the building of Freeport undermined every important political modification in recent Bahamian history."

"Tax haven banking for the purposes of tax evasion and the laundering of illicit monies; resorts featuring casino gambling, apparently owned or managed by organized criminals; and the international traffic in cocaine and marijuana" were the booming industries in 1960s and 1970s Bahamas, Block wrote, run by "the most sophisticated band of criminals this century has produced."

To protect their interests, these men provided campaign financing for political leaders; in particular, those of the newly formed Progressive Liberal Party, the PLP. By 1963, the smell of corruption had lured the IRS to the Caribbean. The American organization deployed several secret agents to investigate the flow of cash in the Bahamas, in an operation known as "Operation Tradewinds."

This was the twisted paradise that attracted Nygard all the way from Canada to its shores.

Initially, Nygard lived on a sailboat during his visits to the Bahamas. He was searching for years for the perfect property to make his Caribbean base. By the mid-seventees, he had found it in an estate he named "Viking Hill." Perched—as the name suggests—on a rolling hill, the home overlooks the clear blue ocean and is surrounded by vibrant tropical flowers and palm trees. Almost anyone would be very grateful to call it home.

For bigger-is-better Nygard, though, it wasn't enough. In the late 1980s, Nygard found another piece of property at the northwestern tip of the island in the exclusive gated community known as Lyford Cay. Nygard claims that actor Sean Connery was his opponent in a bidding war for the beachfront plot, but ultimately the designer walked away the owner. (Connery would go on to build his own Bahamas estate, "Out of Bounds," nearby.)

Nygard felt like his true destiny was beginning to take shape on that beachfront plot of land. He was ready to mold it into his greatest creation so far. "As my aspirations became a reality," Nygard explained, "I began to build my dream home."

Befitting the larger-than-life image he has created for himself, Nygard has insisted for decades that he was the architect of what he called his "magnum opus," despite the fact that he appears to have had no formal architecture or construction training.

"In another life I would have probably been an architect," he once mused. "I love being out there drawing lines and getting my hands dirty."

To be fair, his methods of construction—scribbling what one reporter called "rough sketches" and spray-painting lines on the ground—were "unorthodox."

Over the years and against all odds, the 150,000-square-foot property began to take shape. And what a shape it was.

"This home makes immediate visual contact," Nygard explained in an interview. That was certainly an understatement.

Rising from the tropical foliage, Nygard Cay is anchored by a nearly fifty-foot replica of a Mayan pyramid that was excavated in Tikal, Guatemala. Inside that structure are massive and ornate double doors similar to the infamous Ishtar Gate of Babylon—the main entrance to his lair.

More than three hundred golden and Jamaican palms were planted throughout the grounds, hiding many of the property's structures in the shadows. Below them, gigantic rock sculptures of Mayan warriors and snakes served double duty as gigantic braziers, shooting flames into the night.

(Why the Mayan obsession? Nygard claims that Mayan culture is the closest to the island's ancient indigenous culture. According to historians, however, the island's original inhabitants were Tainos, who were only later influenced by the colonizing Mexican Mayans.)

At the heart of the property was a nearly eighty-foot-tall man-made mountain, supposedly built in the image of the Matterhorn. The tropical version was stocked with climbing vines and a colony of peacocks.

In its shadow were roughly twenty open-plan bedrooms, each with their own name. Nygard spared no expense when it came to these rooms. He told guests that he personally designed all of the beds, which ranged from ten feet long, to twelve feet wide, to octagonal in shape. There was even one that hung on a cable. "By the push of a button, it will lower itself down to the water so you can take a swim with the dolphins," Nygard once explained. "Push the button and go up and have breakfast."

All told, "it pays to sleep around in this place," he once told an interviewer, "because each bedroom is completely different!"

Later, the audacity of that statement would be revealed. Rather than "sleeping around," so many of Nygard's guests were allegedly drugged, raped, and sodomized. Many were virgins at the time of their assaults. The details of all of that, though, wouldn't emerge until later.

In the meantime, the big buzz about Nygard Cay was that it featured bizarre amenities uncommon in the Bahamas and pretty much everywhere else. These are just some of the features that Nygard was happy to show off to guests over the years:

- A three-thousand-CD audio system
- A helipad
- Fake volcanos spurting out dry ice
- An 1,176-square-foot gym built right on the beach, with mirrored doors and a juice bar
- Statues of nude women supposedly modeled on Nygard's exes
- A "disco hut" with cameras under the floors
- Sand that was made right on the property from grinding rocks
- A chunk of the Berlin wall
- A ceiling covered in 100,000 pounds of glass
- 32,000 sq. ft. of entertainment space in the Grand Hall alone
- A sublevel five-star kitchen capable of catering for 800 people
- A dining table to seat twenty-four
- A second dining table, seating thirty-four, that lowered to become the floor of an underground disco
- An underground Mayan-themed cave housing thirty of Nygard's cars
- A racing track that also was used for jogging
- A beachfront volleyball court that hosted Olympic players

- A swimming pool in the house with glass down the middle (Supposedly, there were dolphins on one side and sharks on the other. That alone should tell you something about Nygard's sense of humor.)

"Fundamentally, I am a builder and take great pleasure in seeing my plans evolving and being completed," Nygard explained. "In Nygard Cay, I feel that I am leaving something behind for the Bahamas . . . perhaps even for the world."

Indeed, before long, the world outside of the Bahamas began to take notice. Nygard's property was featured on several episodes of Robin Leach's *Lifestyles of the Rich and Famous*, as well as an ABC special called *Life of Luxury*, hosted by George Hamilton. The home also was featured on Oprah Winfrey's talk show, causing the stunned TV host to exclaim, "I am not living large enough, I reckon!"

Other reported guests to Nygard Cay over the years have included Sean Connery, Robert De Niro, Lenny Kravitz, Michael Jackson, George H. W. Bush, Barbara Bush, Lee Iacocca, Sylvester Stallone, Jessica Alba, and members of the Kennedy clan. (All seem to have had no idea what was really happening there.)

Shockingly Jeffrey Epstein's pal Prince Andrew was even photographed at Nygard Cay *with his children* in tow back in 2000. In photos from the visit, Princesses Eugenie and Beatrice could be seen in matching pink sundresses, as a grinning Nygard stood behind them with his hands on their shoulders. Mom Sarah "Fergie" Ferguson stood off to the side. Another commemorative photo of the visit showed "Randy Andy" deep in conversation with Nygard as the two strolled through the Nygard Cay grounds.

The photos of that visit are not nearly as shocking as the ones that have been the smoking gun for Andrew's relationship with Epstein. For one thing, they were taken in the daytime and there are no young women to be seen— aside from a woman that appears to be Nygard's daughter Bianca. A private investigator who has kept an eye on Nygard for years in the Bahamas told me, "There's nothing really there, as far as that goes. It was just a quick visit. Really a case of wrong place, wrong time for the prince."

(Indeed, at the time Prince Andrew was busy building his relationship with Epstein and his alleged madam, Ghislaine Maxwell. The prince invited the dangerous duo to at least two different royal events in Britain in that year.)

It wasn't just the A-list names that Nygard courted. In the booming early 2000s, Nygard Cay quickly became a playground for lingerie and bikini models flown in from Las Vegas and other major US cities. In July 2008, for example, he hosted "five beautiful models" for a *Playboy* photo shoot, according to an article on "PimpingPhotos.com." A photo from the girls' visit showed one young model playing volleyball in a black nightie, while Nygard rocked a T-shirt that reads: "SHUT UP I'M WORTH A BILLION"

That visit went so well, the models and their handlers would return in September for the "Bringing Sexy Back" three-day weekend in celebration of the "Shirley of Hollywood 60th Anniversary Sexy Model Search Finale." The winner's grand prize would be a photo shoot at Nygard's estate.

Only a few months after that, the girls returned again for the "Racey Girl International Swimsuit & Lingerie Model Search Finals." Nygard was the judge. (The girls named in articles about the event were all of age at the time.) For Nygard, the competition surely wasn't the only highlight. A photographer traveling with the group said that he'd taken thirty thousand photos during their visit. "We shoot models all over the world, and these girls were spectacular," Paul Miller said. "I guarantee you will see the best of these photographs appearing in the pages of the world's top men's magazines." In the meantime, they aimed lower: A photo of Nygard surrounded by four young women in garish lingerie at Nygard Cay graced the cover of the July/August 2009 issue of *Action!* magazine, a publication dedicated to "finding the action in Nevada and California lifestyles."

In the meantime, one model, Maya Rochelle, also filmed the pilot for her TV show *Maya Uncovered* during the visit to Nygard Cay. Several of her lingerie model friends had roles in the show as well. It's unclear if it ever aired.

Nygard gave the local girls opportunities to strut their stuff at Nygard Cay, too. In 2004, he was the judge of the *Caribbean Flava Top Model Search*, a reality show produced by the mysteriously named "N-Tymes Media." Supermodel Beverly Peele, a longtime female friend of Nygard, was a judge as well. (She was also the mother of his son, Trey Peele-Nygard.) For the final episode, the remaining girls were invited to a party at Nygard Cay. According to *Canadian Business* magazine, "At the end of the evening, Rukenya Demeritte, a five-foot, eleven-inch contestant from the PTG Modeling Agency, came out on top, gracefully walking away with the title of Bahamas' Top Model."

The next year, they changed the name of the show to *Bahamas' Top Model* and told local reporters it would be "the most-watched reality show in Bahamas history." Nygard was back as a judge, along with Peele, and another former girlfriend, Yves Lauren, said to be representing "Cleopatra Casting" in New York City. "We promised the contestants opportunities to meet international modeling scouts and we delivered," show producer Donald Knowles told the *Nassau Guardian*. As for Nygard, he had his pick of gorgeous girls to add to the guest list at Nygard Cay.

***

Overall, the time and money that Nygard poured into his Bahamas project was worth it, even if he only spent about six months per year actually there. Asked about the cumulative cost of creating his Mayan playground, Nygard said, "I don't want to know. If I thought too much about price, it might stop me from doing something."

"I know I'm not pissing money away," he insisted. "I'm probably spending 50 cents on the dollar compared to what other people would. Part of the thrill for me is getting good value."

It wasn't the only thrill he found at the Caribbean hideaway.

While outsiders marveled at the over-the-top architecture (and questionable design choices), Nygard Cay began to take on another meaning for locals on the island.

"People used to be saying stuff," a Nassau taxi driver told investigators for this book in March 2020, just weeks after Nygard's New York office was raided.

"They were saying he was having some of these girls come down there, and what he makes them do, and stuff like that. Doing all kinds of stuff . . . Naked, and then he'd say, 'Oh I want that one.'

"I said, 'No, that can't be true.' I didn't believe it. I thought, 'Oh, they probably just don't like him or something like that.'"

But over time, more and more of the island's drivers began to share among themselves what they had seen in their back seats.

"[Girls] would come out of the hotel, catch a cab, and then they would get in," another driver recalled. "He had a secretary or something down there. They'd have the cab number, and they'd call when they needed the girls to come back uptown (to Nassau).

"I never had a conversation with them, only sometimes when they'd go down there, they'd be upset, talking amongst themselves."

Another driver described rumors of "wild parties."

> They were, for the most part, adults who had been taking advantage of kids. When I took anybody there, it was adult females. The only adult person to pick up a kid and take them to Nygard's place would probably be someone on Nygard's payroll.
>
> He had a reputation for giving wild parties. Because of how I grew up, I didn't expect an adult to take advantage of kids. But there are people with money—as I'm sure you know—who think they can buy anything and get away with anything, and they take advantage.
>
> The women would have their names on a sheet that the security guard could check. If somebody wanted me to pick them up at a certain time, they'd leave my name and the taxi number at the gate, so I wouldn't have any problem getting in.

Yet another driver, one of the few female drivers on the island, actually was an invited guest to Nygard Cay years ago.

"It comes off like, 'Hey! Peter Nygard is having a party. Would you like to go?'" she recalled over lunch with investigators for this book at the Arawak Cay fish fry.

> If you're my friend, and you say, "Would you like to go to a party?'
> You would say, 'Yeah!"
> Then they say, "Well, it's at Nygard's. . ."
> I'm thinking, "Hmmm maybe I don't wanna be a part of that."
> Parties at Nygard's go on not for one day. It's a weekend, or the whole week.
> You could only get in there through an invite.
> You're going to go, "What an opportunity! I'd like to model."
> You can probably meet certain people there, stuff like that.
> My instinct was, I don't wanna be a part of that. And I had three older brothers who would kill me. I turned it down.

Community activist Reverend C. B. Moss said few people at the time could even imagine the allegations to come. "I'd heard, you know, rumors," he said in an interview for this book, "but not in such explicit detail and certainly not in the horrendous nature of the alleged acts . . . the fact that all these children were being involved."

Tragically, even those who had a front-row seat to the constant flow of girls to Nygard's home turned a blind eye thanks to cultural standards that devalued young women.

"Many of the drivers used to drop girls down there," an older female driver told our team. "But then I say, you know, if you don't know what you're going for, why are you going to that house? Why are you catching taxis to go there? And then you decide, 'OK, he raped me.' I'm a little skeptical about that raping business, because what are you doing there in the first place?"

Many others in Nassau and its outskirts told our team that they shared a similar opinion. But what those adults failed to take into account is that many of the women heading to Nygard Cay—some allegedly as young as fourteen years old—were sheltered, naive, and utterly unprepared for what they would find there.

Moss said it best: "It's a subject that carries with it a certain degree of shame and degradation and people feel, 'Well, if I wasn't there or whatever, it would not have happened.' So it's self blaming. We need to encourage people to come forward with the understanding that no one has the right. Even if you accept an invitation to a party, no one has a right to take that kind of liberty with you."

Our investigative team spoke to one woman who learned that lesson the hard way. She told her story on the condition of anonymity, still fearful of how far Nygard's reach still extends on the island.

"I definitely can say I worked," she began. "They called it 'work.'" She remembers being somewhere between seventeen and nineteen at the time.

"I did every weekend for about a year," she said. "Normally when you go, your name is put on a list so you can attend next week and then they would call you Thursday or Friday to let you know that, 'Hey, your name is on the list so we're expecting to see you.' For me it was in about 2002 to 2003."

During that period in the Bahamas, Nygard was known to be throwing parties almost every weekend. "He would have girls that were invited, politicians, police officers," the woman remembered. "You know, persons of high caliber. Local and international individuals."

"They called them 'pamper parties,' for the most part," she said. "Get your massage. Get your nails done. They'd get you a drink, make sure that you eat. They didn't really want you to wear clothes, so they'd give you skimpy swimsuits, or a top and a small skirt or something like that. As revealing as possible."

Before long, she claimed, the reason for that dress code would become woefully apparent.

"Someone would come over to you and say, 'XYZ would like to have a conversation.' Or, 'This person would like to get to know you better.' Or, 'I would want you to go entertain this person,'" she claimed. "Stuff like that."

Once introduced, "They would go off in a room, or you go in the jacuzzi with them," she claimed. "Everything is a pair situation. To be honest, it's like one big orgy"

One night, the woman—then just a teen—caught Nygard's eye.

She claimed, "He took me into his bedroom and he was like . . . 'If you keep doing this with me, I can make you out to be somebody that's constantly a part of my fashion line.' Modeling was one of the things he used to—I guess you can say—attract the attention of young women. So that was kind of a way he got you in." The woman says she declined, intending to make her way in the world on her own terms. If a girl like her refused Nygard's advances, though, there was always next time.

"He would tell you, 'Oh next week we're doing this again, so you can bring a friend,'" she claimed. "'Make sure she looks like you: tall, slim, etc.' You would bring your friends, but you weren't allowed to bring any male friends. Strictly female. The local males were not allowed on the grounds unless they worked for him or were in the high society like politicians or police officers that he would bring in.

"I was one of those that walked away from the situation relatively early. I was not into the idea of having sex be my entrance into the world of modeling."

In fact, the woman told our investigators that she did get some modeling experience at Nygard Cay—no strings attached.

"For me, I was never pressured," she said. "He had these amateur boxing matches, and I was asked several times to be the ring girl. The boxing matches served to get everybody relaxed and into the scenery and they would break off after the first two matches or so."

"Most of these girls were still in school," she alleged. "We're talking high school girls where two or three or maybe $500 seems like a lot of money for them, so they'd go for it."

Over time, the whole scene lost its luster.

"Also, I saw quite a few politicians at one point, and that surprised me," she said. "Like, you guys are supposed to be protecting us, our well-being as citizens. But you're here and allowing this person who has money, you're allowing him to basically take advantage of the situation. That for me, as young as I was, that for me kind of really resonated with me.

"It was not something that I was accustomed to," she continued. "At one point I started thinking as an individual, and I decided to bring my friend and his brother there, and that apparently was against the rules, because you weren't allowed to bring males there. You were only allowed to bring females.

"[Nygard] said that he'd had enough of me doing it. I said, 'You know, I'm sure I'll see you,' . . . but after me bringing my friend and his brother on to the scene I was taken off the list."

***

For outsiders and visitors, it was clear that something unusual was going at Nygard Cay. Second- and thirdhand rumors ran wild throughout the Bahamian community for nearly twenty years, according to locals. No one seemed to know the entire truth, but the lucky ones knew enough to stay away.

For Nygard and his powerful pals, that was probably how they wanted to keep things. It was only those inside Nygard's innermost circle who knew the full extent of the events unfurling at Nygard Cay. Dependent on his paychecks and in fear of Nygard's powerful friends, they weren't about to start talking—at least, not yet.

CHAPTER 5
BETRAYAL

Does he even still have a conscience?
—Richette Ross

Richette Ross was a single mom living with her two children in a small room in Nassau when she first heard of Peter Nygard. Trained as a masseuse, she was asked to come out to Nygard Cay and treat the billionaire to a session. Besides the fact that the treatment took place in a gigantic Mayan party palace, Ross could tell from the start that this would be no ordinary job.

Ross claimed in an interview recorded for this book that while she was massaging Nygard, everything seemed to be proceeding like normal. Then, as she was finishing up, he demanded that she massage his "third leg." Ross claims she brushed it off, and continued picking up her things.

"When I got downstairs," she said, there was another Nygard employee "informing me I was hired."

Despite that early red flag, it was an offer that Ross couldn't refuse. "In my mind," she explained, 'the only thing I was thinking was providing for my kids." Ross swallowed her doubts and took the job, vowing to protect herself at all costs.

"My job was to be on call" for massages, she said. In the beginning, it seemed like it could be the opportunity of a lifetime.

"We had talk show hosts, lawyers, doctors" visiting the "breathtaking" property, she said. "And the pay was great."

Of course, like so many other Nygard employees, Ross claims her job soon became a living hell.

"My job shifted shortly before I became household manager," Ross continued. "My duties as household manager was to oversee the setup . . . to make sure that the girls have everything they need, to buy supplies for them," and to coordinate Nygard's infamous "pamper parties."

Said Ross, "*Everything* happened at the pamper parties."

According to Nygard's right-hand woman, Nygard staffers used Facebook posts and messages to promote upcoming parties, which offered "free dinners, massages, pedicures, and boat rides" to guests—"mainly females," said Ross. "Mr. Nygard didn't like the competition."

Once the party began, though, Nygard would kick off a twisted competition of his own, she claimed. As guests arrived, they would be photographed and entered into Nygard's personal database. He even rated them upon entry, Ross claimed: A, B, C, or D, with A being the most beautiful. A local investigator told me he had personally seen this database.

What were Nygard's ranking criteria? Ross claimed the women had to have what Nygard called "a nice toilet . . . a nice ass. It had to be big and round." In addition, company communications filed in court revealed that girls wouldn't "be let in if they are big-boned."

Pamper parties often kicked off in the daytime, lending an air of harmless gaiety to the proceedings. All that shifted as night fell.

Ross claimed, "Throughout the day, he'd ask a particular girl if she'd like to stay the night."

If she said no? Ross alleged, "Then there's always drugging."

Ross said in an interview recorded for this book that she personally witnessed one of Nygard's bartenders drop a pill into a girl's drink after hiding it between his fingers.

"He just dropped it," Ross alleged. "She took the cup and left."

"Around 10:00, we were almost ready to shut down," Ross claimed, when she spotted the girl again. "She was crying . . . naked . . . in the office. Disorientated."

Tragically, according to Ross, this wasn't an unusual occurrence. She claimed, "It happened often." She even said that at least once, she saw a girl "escape" from the property, only to be brought back by Bahamian police, apparently against her will.

Little did Ross know, she would soon personally experience what she before had only witnessed. For years, Ross had settled into an easy comfort with Nygard. She had come to view him as more of a paternal figure than a predator.

"We had a relationship where it was pretty transparent," Ross said in her interview. "He would share things with me.

"I thought I had a relationship with him where he wouldn't hurt me." Like a lion, he had lured her into a sense of safety. Ross says that before long, he was ready to pounce.

It was a day like any other when Ross was summoned to give Nygard his usual coconut oil massage. "His skin," she said, "was always dry."

As she went about her work, Ross claimed, Nygard's girlfriend offered her a glass of wine. It seemed unusual, and she declined the offer to focus on her work.

Still, Ross said, "She stopped me and insisted I have that glass of wine."

"As I was going up the stairs . . . he was on the phone to politicians with the girlfriend I had seen in the kitchen," Ross continued.

"I felt a warmness coming over my body. I turned to tell him I wasn't feeling good. I remember going down.

"When I came to," Ross alleged, "he was penetrating me. I could see from the mirror (on the ceiling). I knew he was on top of me.

"I remember trying to ease my way to the edge of the bed."

The rest, even now, is just a blur. Six years later, you can still hear the pain and shame in Ross's voice when she talks about it. The hesitation to reveal each painful detail. Still, in the cloud of emotion surrounding the incident, there's one thing Ross said she knows for sure: "He raped me."

"When I came back downstairs, the look on the other girls' faces . . . I could see what happened to me had happened to them," she said. "I felt nasty. I felt dirty."

Ross finally quit working for Nygard in 2014, the paycheck no longer worth what she had to endure to get it.

"After I left, he would call my cell," she claimed. "I wouldn't answer."

For years, her memories of that day were a dark and painful secret. She struggled with carrying not only the truth about what happened to her, but the memories of everything else she had witnessed at Nygard Cay. Could she have been the whistleblower to take it all down? Could she have stopped him? Ross was and is skeptical that real change ever could have happened with the police and the government under Nygard's thumb.

"Who was I going to report to?" Ross asked. "I couldn't tell anybody what happened. There's no laws here. These people aren't gonna do anything. Who do you even go to?"

Ross finally found support in a local nonprofit organization founded to help sexual violence victims, known as Sanctuary.

"I am grateful for Sanctuary," Ross said. "They gave the Bahamian girls a voice. This time, we will be heard."

Sanctuary helped Ross and some of the other victims get back on their feet with financial support and sometimes even arranged housing. Unbelievably, Nygard's team has pointed to this fact as evidence the girls were paid off to lie about their interactions with Nygard. The organization is partly funded by at least one person who has tussled with Nygard in the past. Focusing on that fact, though, is losing sight of the forest for the trees.

At the end of the day, the organization provided much-needed resources to an incredibly victimized and traumatized segment of the Bahamian population, when no one else would do so. Asking for help and receiving it should not make their allegations any less believable.

As for Ross, she said that the organization provided her with the support and protection she needed to summon the courage to speak out against one of the Bahamas' most powerful men. Ross even became a sort of leader in the community, introducing other alleged victims to the organization in the hopes of getting them therapy and the community support they'd never had.

Before long, though, Ross had made herself a target.

"At one point, I was basically in hiding," she alleged, describing threats that were issued "all the time."

"I knew too much," Ross explained.

She even has alleged that Nygard went so far as to kill her family dog. The *New York Times* found that Nygard actually wired her $10,000 at one point, emailing Ross: "I sent you money to buy a new dog." (He blamed the dog's death on a political rival.)

Adding threats and persecution to the trauma of her past made life even more challenging for Ross, she said. Remembering and retelling her story is now a painful cycle that has taken over her days. All these years later, she can't seem to escape the specter of Nygard.

"He took away my entire life," she said, sadly, wondering, "Does he even still have a conscience?"

***

AUTHOR'S NOTE ON RICHETTE ROSS & OTHER VICTIMS

Nygard's attorney has insisted that Ross has "no credibility whatsoever" because she's been "paid off" to tell her story and to recruit other victims to tell theirs. For her part, Ross has passed a polygraph test that confirmed she never paid anyone to lie about Nygard.

Ross has accepted money throughout her fight to find justice, which she says was for her time and expenses in reaching out to other victims. Other victims told reporters for the *New York Times* that they received payments in the process of coming forward to speak out as well. The *Times* called these payments "vulnerabilities," implying that the women were less believable because they had taken money (supposedly from one of Nygard's enemies) in the process of telling their darkest secrets.

No sources were paid for their contributions to this book. Throughout my career, however, I have worked for organizations that do pay sources—a practice highly frowned upon by traditional organizations like the *New York*

Times. That paper's ethics guidelines insist that "to do so would give sources incentive to falsify material."

As reporters, we parachute into the lives of people who are very often grappling with the most traumatic experiences of their lives. We ask them to dig into their wounds and to share their stories with complete strangers simply out of a desire to see the truth told to the world. We wring them dry of their tears, blast their secrets out to the world, and fly back to our fast-paced media lives. The best of us stay in touch, checking in to see how they are weathering the fallout. In the end, though, they are left behind to pick up the pieces.

Most sources are indeed incredibly altruistic, and do want to see truth shared and justice served. It can be overwhelming to see their bravery and resolve firsthand. Journalists are supposed to be driven by that desire as well. Today, there are many citizen journalists and online renegades who investigate, analyze, and report purely for the joy of it. When it comes to multimillion-dollar organizations like the *Times*, though, money is a big incentive to tell the best story first.

No matter how pure reporters think their motives may be, they and their organizations profit from the most painful secrets of regular people. (Incidentally, that is often an incentive for journalists to falsify material, as we saw with Jayson Blair and Stephen Glass.) Of course, journalism costs money to execute, and we need to make a living. It's an argument I've made on my own behalf in the past.

But why shouldn't the people who actually experienced the heartbreak of these major stories be compensated for their time and their role in the journalistic process, too?

At the end of the day, there are countless incentives for a source to falsify material—none of which involve money. A source might carry a grudge against the person they are exposing in a newspaper's pages. They might want their "fifteen minutes of fame," a link they can share with friends on their Facebook page. They might be starstruck by the dazzling aura of celebrity reporters like Ronan Farrow, and eager to forge a connection with the

A-list by reaching out with their story. The motivations for moving from a regular citizen to an integral cog in the media machine are legion.

Journalists navigate all of these extenuating factors with every source and every story. It's a key part of the job: We must wade through the swamp of external forces to uncover the grains of truth within it. That means finding corroboration in the form of documents or secondary sources. It means cross-checking and verifying every detail. Above all, it means being conscious of the reasons why a particular individual might embellish or alter the truth. We do it every day, with every story. If we are able to do that successfully with so many outside factors, why can't we do that with source payments? It all seems like a convenient excuse for media organizations to take one more item off of their expense list.

As with Harvey Weinstein and Bill Cosby before him, the case of Peter Nygard is a he said / she said, she said, she said, she said, she said. Reporters know that where there's smoke, there's often fire. The more women, across continents and decades, who share the same story, the more likely it is that it's true.

Having met these victims, and heard them tell their stories themselves, I know that anyone experienced in dealing with victims of trauma would be inclined to believe that they are telling the truth. Trauma specialists know that it is very difficult for people to consistently fake trauma responses. (As a woman, it's hard to imagine what amount of money it would take to fake being a rape victim for years, with oceans of tears on demand along the way.)

I have heard these women break down in tears while telling their stories. I have heard the fear and shame that still chokes their throats as they try to force out the memories of their darkest moments.

I believe the victims.

In the meantime, Nygard "needs to be brought to justice," Richette Ross said in the interview recorded for this book. "He needs to be jailed."

She continued, "I want people to know that what's now breaking, there's still other things" that happened.

CHAPTER 6
SOMETHING TO HIDE

I was brave enough to do things in a different way.
—Peter Nygard

In 2009, recession-weary New York City was hit with a marketing meteorite. Peter Nygard was opening up a massive, futuristic concept store in the heart of Times Square, with a giant poster out front that taunted passersby: "We decided not to join the recession."

In fact, press releases issued by Nygard's company at the time bragged that the company had grown more than 25 percent in recent months, surpassing $1 billion in revenue.

"This businessman is doing fine while the rest of the world is coughing," one release boasted. "When the US sneezes, the world catches a cold."

Instead, Nygard claimed it was business as usual for him, bragging, "I enjoy the fruits of my success."

Little did he know that a storm was brewing, one with the power to take down his business, his reputation, and his public image once and for all.

While Nygard was pumping out his over-the-top recession-proof PR, reporters for the Canadian Broadcasting Company (CBC) were quietly speaking with former Nygard employees and other insiders about their experiences working with Canada's most infamous man. At the grand opening of his Manhattan store on November 6, 2009, a CBC reporter even showed up with a cameraman in tow.

The material they gathered was explosive. Slowly but surely, the company put it all together as a bombshell episode of the CBC documentary series, *Fifth Estate*. The episode, "Larger Than Life," was scheduled to air on April 10, 2010. But Nygard wasn't going down without a fight.

Only weeks after his grand opening, Nygard filed a lawsuit in the US District Court against the CBC, claiming that their uninvited reporter had recorded his restricted event and had therefore performed copyright infringement. It was certainly a creative way to go after the CBC, but Nygard was fired up, and just beginning.

That same month, the Nygard International Partnership filed an application in San Jose, California, attempting to subpoena Google. Nygard wanted to force them to reveal the identity of someone who posted on the entertainment blog www.shesomajor.com on November 12, 2009. (Needless to say, Google was not especially forthcoming.)

The biggest bombshell, though, was the suit that Nygard filed in Canada against the CBC and several former employees who had spoken to the network for their special. According to Nygard, the CBC had broken the law on several fronts. First, he claimed that reporters had "harassed" many of his employees at their homes in an attempt to get them to participate in the show. The CBC's methods of reporting were allegedly so outrageous, eight Nygard employees filed complaints against the network.

A rep for Nygard claimed in court documents that the CBC "improperly conspired with and encouraged the employees to release confidential information to" the network, including passenger lists from his private jet, aircraft manifests, confidential emails and video of company-related activities at Nygard Cay. In addition, he claimed, the employees' very statements to the CBC were in violation of confidentiality agreements they had signed as new hires for Nygard.

Worse, Nygard said, the sources featured in the show were by their very nature untrustworthy. "The CBC defendants know that . . . embittered former employees are unreliable sources of information who have their own axes to grind," the lawsuit claimed. He called the ex-employees' statements "defamatory, false, and malicious," part of a wider "vendetta" meant to bring him down.

According to Nygard's attorney, the supposed campaign of destruction was working. "This has caused an enormous amount of damage to our client," attorney Richard Good said, "at a time when management personnel should be devoting all their energies to protecting the business and its employees from the effects of the economic recession."

The goal of the lawsuit was not just to prevent the show from airing; the ultimate goal was silence and intimidation. Nygard's attorneys said in court filings that they hoped to prevent the CBC and his former employees "from disclosing, divulging, and conveying to any person or entity Nygard's confidential information and from encouraging or inducing any existing or former Nygard employee from doing so."

In response, Richard Kravetsky—an attorney for one of the defendants—blasted that Nygard was "suing former employees for telling the truth." For their part, the CBC warned the court that the very identity of the Canadian nation was at stake. (Much like the American Constitution, Canada's Charter of Rights and Freedoms defends the freedom of speech and press. Unlike the Constitution, the Charter was created relatively recently in 1982, and is therefore even more vulnerable than our frequently challenged American document.)

"I consider these actions and demands . . . as an attempt to intimidate and frighten sources of information for a journalism investigation about a matter of public interest," CBC Managing Editor Cecil Rosner said in an affidavit. "I am also concerned that this action and the attempted interference with CBC's investigation may have a chilling effect on the willingness of individuals to speak with journalists and producers about the matters being researched and investigated."

In a victory for free press—albeit a temporary one—the show aired as planned on April 9, 2010, on the CBC. The show's TV guide summary read as follows:

His name is Peter Nygard. Almost everything about him seems larger than life. There's the fashion business that clothes millions of women that's made him one of the richest people in Canada. Then there's his palatial tropical estate and the lavish lifestyle he lives there.

Over the years, Peter Nygard's image as a public figure has been carefully crafted: The self-made man, the corporate visionary, the Olympic athlete, and the philanthropist with awards declaring him an exemplary Canadian. It's all part of the Nygard brand.

But for some who've worked for him inside his company, behind that public image there's another Peter Nygard. What happened to them raises issues that are often hidden by silence and secrecy: about workplace bullying and harassment and the toll they can take.

"The truth has to come out," says Pat Prowse, a former Director of Human Resources with the company. "And people need to know what they are supporting when they buy those products."

According to the CBC show, people buying Nygard clothing were supporting mismanagement of employees, illegal business practices, and even possibly sex with underage women.

The heart of the documentary's most explosive claims centered around a Florida couple who had previously worked for Nygard at Nygard Cay—Allan and Michelle May. The Mays had battled with Nygard in court back in 2005, over claims that he was withholding their wages—and worse.

Nygard said the Mays's claims were outrageously defamatory, and noted that the two were convicted con artists with a history of making false claims. (They were convicted in 2009 on a civil fraud claim, according to newspaper reports out of the Caribbean.) However, it was Nygard's own words that made the biggest splash for the show.

The *Fifth Estate* posted several clips of Nygard's depositions in his 2005 case against the Mays online—clips that showed him admitting to business practices that were far outside of the norm, to say the least.

One clip opens with Nygard telling the gathered employees about his practice of fining employees. Taking money out of employees' wages is illegal in the Bahamas.

"Only thing seems to work with these people is money," Nygard sniffed, explaining his policy of fining workers for lapses in job performance. Insisting he knew that taking money out of an employee's pay was illegal, Nygard said it was "taken out of bonus money, the tip money, if you like."

The deposition video continued as the Mays' attorney cited one example when a Bahamian employee was "fined $25 for a dirty glass at the beach cabana."

"His job was to clean glass," Nygard responded, nonplussed, "and that was what he was brought in to do. So I guess he didn't clean the glass."

In another incident, a Nygard Cay employee named Maxwell was fined $25 because someone found several tiny mosquitos known as no-see-ums in an area that was under his care.

"So his job was to do the spraying correctly and do the mouse and the rat traps and No-See-Ums, which is a very nasty mosquito . . . bug control and so this was his particular job," Nygard explained, insisting the fee was warranted. He didn't seem to see anything wrong with such heavy fines for such small offenses.

Another employee, according to the video, was fined because some houseflies were spotted in Nygard Cay's Grand Hall.

Taking that money out of the employees' wages would have been illegal—not to mention heartless. Nygard insisted the punishments only affected their bonuses, but the attorney for Alan and Michelle Mays told Nygard in the deposition that he had proof that showed that wasn't how it happened.

Producing an old pay stub for a Bahamian employee named "Woody," the attorney had Nygard confirm that the man had worked fifty-three hours between May 8 and May 21, for a total of $321. Nygard nodded.

"Now, he had $275 deducted in his pay," the attorney said. "Isn't that what it shows in deductions from gross?"

Nygard replied, "So it seems to, yeah."

"Why would he have had $275 in fines taken out of his pay for a two-week period?" the attorney asked.

Squinting at the paper, Nygard said, "I think she made a mistake here."

"If you go down to net pay, it's $46," the attorney continued. "If in fact he only got $46 for those fifty-three hours, that would not comply with Bahamian minimum wage law would it?" (In 2001, the Bahamian Minimum wage law set the minimum wage at $4 per hour. It's gone up since then, to $5.25 in 2020.)

Nygard admitted that the paycheck seemed out of compliance, but insisted that it was simply a typographical error.

A similar issue came to light when the attorney presented Nygard with a loan document for an employee at Nygard Cay, one Angela Grant.

"You, in effect, in this document lent Angela Grant $250 for two weeks, and another $250 for a total of four weeks, and you charged her 4.8 percent of that total amount as part of the loan," the attorney explained. "That's an equivalent interest rate at about 80 percent per annum."

"Those were her numbers," Nygard insisted. "We charged her what she wanted to get the loan for. . . . She considered it a great big favor."

"We don't have a loan program for maids and people unless they really have an emergency, and she offered to pay this kind of interest back and we just agreed to it and she signed it accordingly."

Changing tacks, Nygard said, "That arrangement was made between her and [the former director of human resources] at the end of the day, not me. I would never have anything to do with interest rates myself."

The attorney reminded Nygard that the maximum interest rate for such a loan in the Bahamas would be 20 percent per annum—far below the 80 percent he had charged. Still, Nygard brushed it off, insisting it had been a clerical oversight and not an illegal agreement.

The attorney then confronted Nygard with a third major employment issue, explaining how thirteen men were arrested by immigration in the Bahamas on October 3, 2003, supposedly en route to work at Nygard Cay and with no work permits to be found. Nygard insisted that to his knowledge, all employees had always been permitted. Any that hadn't had been pulling the wool over his eyes, he insisted.

All of those allegations, while somewhat unusual and ethically shaky, paled in comparison to the Mays couple's biggest bombshell: the implication that he'd flown in an underage Dominican girl to be his birthday "present" at a Nygard Cay bash.

Fifth Estate host Bob McKeown coyly described the arrival of a "special package" from the Dominican Republic for Nygard's birthday party in 2003. The Mays then claimed on air that they had later found the girl—who they said was underage—panicked and screaming on the property.

This allegation was at the heart of a defamation lawsuit Nygard filed against the CBC and several of its employees in 2012. Not only were the allegations "untrue and defamatory," Nygard said in the suit; but also, he claimed that the CBC had been provided with a notarized statement from the woman the day before the show aired, insisting that she had been an adult when she visited Nygard Cay, and that nothing untoward had happened. In addition, Nygard's girlfriend at the time had told the CBC that he'd spent every night in his private cabana with her throughout the period during which the woman had been visiting. Still, the CBC aired the allegations.

That lawsuit was only Nygard's first volley of return fire. He dragged the CBC, its reporters, and his former employees through court for the next several years, even hiring an ex–Scotland Yard investigator to dig up the network's secrets. As recently as 2019, a judge placed a temporary stay on the proceedings in one case. Today, no footage from the episode remains online, and even descriptions of what it included are hard to uncover.

Still, just days after the *Fifth Estate* episode aired, another media storm was descending. On April 14, 2010, the National Labor Committee issued a press release with this bombshell headline: "Women's Clothing Lines for Nygard/Dillard's, JC Penney & Wal-Mart Linked To Human Trafficking in Jordan Sweatshop"

The NLC was founded in 1980 to "defend human and worker rights globally." In Nygard, it seemed they had found an egregious offender. According to the NLC, Nygard's women's clothing line was at least partially produced at the International British Garments (IBG) factory, located just one hour outside Amman, Jordan. There, in a nondescript beige brick building, more than 1,200 guest workers from Southeast Asian nations such as Sri Lanka, Bangladesh, and India sewed together Nygard's creations. At least 75 percent of the workers were women. All of them, the NLC claimed, had "been trafficked to Jordan, stripped of their passports and held under conditions of indentured servitude."

Life inside the factory was a living hell, according to NLC Director Charles Kernaghan. He described "all-night 23-hour shifts, from 7 a.m. to 6 a.m. at least once a week." Kernaghan continued, "The exhausted workers are at the factory over 110 hours a week, while being cheated of over half the legal wages due them. Instead of earning the 74.5-cents-an-hour minimum wage in Jordan, they are paid just 35 cents an hour." Absurdly, the release claims, workers were paid about 9 cents per pair of pants they completed. Back in the U.S., the pants retailed for $38.

When it was finally time to rest, the workers got little reprieve. "Workers are housed in filthy primitive dormitories without heat and with only sporadic access to water for two hours, three or four days a week," the release claimed, and the dorms were "infested with bed bugs."

Allegedly, it was a nightmare that was incredibly difficult—if not impossible—for the workers to escape. "When workers ask for the return of their passports and to be paid correctly, they are slapped and threatened with forcible deportation," said Kernaghan "There are also serious allegations of sexual harassment, even rape, and of workers being worked to death."

At the time, a Nygard rep claimed that "a government inquiry found no truth to the allegations." The workers were hopeful that Nygard would not pack up his business and leave them searching for more work. In fact, seven months later *Forbes* reported that the NLC revealed factory conditions "improved significantly" after their publicity campaign. "Passports have been returned, and workers now get Fridays off," *Forbes* said. Nygard's plane was spotted flying into Jordan as recently as 2017.

The Jordan "sweatshop" scandal blew over relatively quickly, but it wouldn't be Nygard's last. Just over a year later, there was trouble brewing at another factory linked to his clothing line—this time in Cambodia.

According to a documentary called *Apparel Truth*, more than five hundred workers walked out of the Nan Kuang Garment factory on August 4, 2011, in protest over poor working conditions. A reporter for the documentary claimed that the labor abuses in the facility, which produced Nygard clothing, were shocking.

Just outside of the factory, the documentary crew interviewed a young worker who claimed to be 15. "They illegally take these girls on in exchange for cheaper labor costs," the narrator says. A typical work schedule at that time was ten to twelve hours per day, six days per week, they claimed, and workers made roughly $30 per month in salary. There was no paid sick leave.

Nygard's Cambodian partners came under fire again in July 2017, when the international activist group Clean Clothes Campaign announced that workers at a factory producing Nygard items were claiming they were owed more than half a million dollars in back wages.

According to the organization's report, customs data showed "substantial shipments to Nygard" from a Cambodian factory called Chung Fai between November 2015 and April 2016. Chung Fai shut down in July 2016, the report said, leaving workers owed more than $500,000 in unpaid back wages.

When approached about the claims, a rep for Nygard seemed to suggest that they could only control so much of what went on at their production partners' facilities. Production partners were required to sign a document swearing they would respect Nygard's worker rights standards, the rep claimed, and the company regularly checked in on the factories to ensure they were still in compliance. With so many factories around the world, it seemed, some workers were falling through the cracks.

It's an issue that's dogged him for decades. As recently as 2018, he was criticized for producing clothes in Myanmar, where the Muslim Rohingya people continue to face vicious persecution. A columnist for the *Cape Breton Spectator* was stunned to find out her snazzy new top had come from such a place. "What I really found unbelievable is that Peter Nygård, the company's founder and head, would set up shop in a country where human rights are trampled, where the military has destroyed villages," and worse, columnist Dorothy Campbell wrote.

In the end, she decided, "To buy or not to buy is an ethical dilemma, given that so many long-suffering workers depend on their meager salaries to live even at a subsistence level, while Nygård receives stem cell injections, parties on and laughs all the way to the bank. Perhaps he skips his way to the bank after the injections. All I know for sure that nothing 'Made in Myanmar' will adorn my ageing body."

The specter of impropriety has always followed Nygard—even, it seems, when it might not be deserved. In some ways, his taste for a good legal fight has probably brought more attention to his various scandals than they otherwise would have earned. Still, the man has admitted himself that he makes his own rules. In the Bahamas, he found the perfect playground for his dark side.

CHAPTER 7
FRIENDS IN LOW PLACES

I love Bahamian black people!
— Peter Nygard

Political corruption in the Bahamas is almost as old as the palm trees and the sand beneath them. Not long after his arrival on the island, Nygard began to insinuate himself into that ecosystem, cultivating relationships with the local authorities and stakeholders.

In particular, Nygard aligned himself with the Progressive Liberal Party (PLP), which came back into power in the 2002 general election. According to an American diplomatic cable from that period, the election had been suffused by millions of shady campaign contributions from "questionable sources."

Once in power, the PLP began siding with Nygard in his fight to grow the footprint of his Nygard Cay property. Their time in power, however, would be limited to one term after an explosive scandal rocked the island—one involving another larger-than-life blonde, Nygard's girlfriend Anna Nicole Smith.

***

Tall, blonde, and busty, Smith was certainly Nygard's type. When they first met in the late 1990s at his annual Academy Awards bash, she was just in her late 20s and still in the prime of her career. (She was also a newly minted heiress, hot off the 1995 death of her nonagenarian petroleum mogul husband J. Howard Marshall.)

The two dated from 1997 to 2000, and Smith even modeled for Nygard's fashion line in between trips to Nygard Cay. A blown-up photo of her with Nygard graced the walls of his N-Force jet for years.

"She was truly a sweetheart," Nygard told Fox News anchor Rita Cosby for her book, *Blonde Ambition: The Untold Story Behind Anna Nicole Smith's Death*.

"One of the most fun, charming people you would ever meet," he remembered. "But she had such a problem with drugs. I thoroughly enjoyed her when she was sober, but I was so depressed when I saw her so drunk and out of it."

Nygard told Cosby that he often put Smith in a separate hotel room when they traveled, so he wouldn't have to see her intoxicated. He also allegedly assigned her a minder whenever she visited Nygard Cay, out of fears that she would fall into a lagoon or otherwise injure herself on the sprawling grounds of the property.

For health-obsessed Nygard, it all grew to be too much. Nygard claimed he eventually told her, "You are not going to self-destruct on my watch," and broke it off by 2000. Instead, she would self-destruct in front of the entire world starting in 2002, on E's *The Anna Nicole Show*. In the show, the world was exposed to the most garish and tragic details of the former model's fall from grace. Far from the nail in the coffin of her public image, though, the show proved to be a launching point for a new era of Smith's life and career.

After a deal with Trimspa diet pills, Smith had slimmed down and fattened her wallet. Her behavior was still raising red flags about her sobriety, but by 2006, she was pregnant with her second child and ready to retire in the tropical paradise she had visited so often with Nygard.

Nygard claimed, "Anna called me twice before she came to the Bahamas, around June of 2006. She told me she may be going there, and she told me she was looking for a house." Nygard said he told her he was too busy with work to play host, but she found a soft landing at the oceanside estate of her ex, South Carolina developer Ben Thompson, a property called Horizons.

Smith gave birth to her daughter Dannielynn on September 7, 2006. Her son, Daniel, arrived from the United States to see his new sister two days later. On September 10, he was found dead in Anna Nicole's hospital bed, from an accidental overdose of methadone and antidepressants. The story of what happened there is a whole other book.

For the purposes of Nygard's tale, what really matters is that Smith was desperately fighting at this time to establish residency in the Bahamas. She had a host of legal and financial reasons, but mainly, she wanted to keep her ex Larry Birkhead from trying to get custody or visitation rights with newborn Dannielynn. To that end, Smith and her associates struck up a relationship with Minister of Immigration and Labor Shane "Shameless" Gibson, a prominent member of the PLP and an associate of Nygard's.

Not long after Smith connected with Gibson, her residency permit was issued, seemingly out of the blue. It had taken just three weeks, when normal applicants normally wait years—and the locals noticed. As editorial columnists questioned the nature of that transaction, Gibson was thrust into the spotlight. Allegations of corruption flew. One report claimed that he had accepted a $10,000 bribe, a Rolex, and other gifts from Smith and her team to fast-track her application. He insisted there were "never any gifts for favors," a statement at least one local newspaper found to be suspiciously worded.

Still, the nature of Gibson's relationship with Smith would come under close scrutiny after her sudden and scandalous death in a Florida hotel room on February 8, 2007. (The wife of Gibson's dad, Brigitte, was the one who found Smith's body.)

Smith's death didn't end Gibson's problems. Days after her passing, on February 12, 2007, the front page of the Bahamian *Tribune* blasted news of a photo exclusive: "Shane & Anna Nicole: The Dramatic New Photos." Splashed across the broadsheet were several disturbing photos of Gibson in bed with Smith (both fully clothed) surrounded by pink flowers and white ribbon in her bedroom. In one garish photo, they gazed into each other's eyes. Gibson grinned at the camera; Smith appeared to be seriously out of it.

Fallout for Gibson was swift. "He should do the right thing and step down," Cassius Stuart, a member of a rival political party told reporters, insisting Gibson had "shamed" the entire nation of the Bahamas. Gibson did indeed resign before the end of the month. That wouldn't be the end of his political career though, if Peter Nygard had any say in it.

In the meantime, shock waves continued to ripple through Nassau and beyond. Far from just a celebrity scandal, the incident had far-reaching implications for the Bahamian political landscape. In March 2007, Reuters reported, "Opposition leaders charged that the government's handling of Smith's case shows its incompetence," noting that the race between Gibson's PLP party (supported by Nygard), and the Free National Movement (FNM) had tightened.

Ultimately, when the polls closed on May 2, 2007, the FNM emerged victorious, with 49.86 percent of the vote to the PLP's 47.02 percent. The scandal, it seemed, had booted the PLP from power.

When the general election rolled around again a few years later, Nygard made it his mission to get Gibson and the PLP back on top. Campaign finance laws in the Bahamas are flexible, to say the least, so none of Nygard's political pals were required to disclose any of the payments that he received from him—or anyone else. Still, the details of their arrangements were kept relatively hush-hush.

Former Nygard employee Richette Ross said in an interview recorded for this book claimed that she was personally tasked with putting together payoffs for high-ranking PLP members.

"Nygard loved anybody he could manipulate," she claimed, explaining how she saw "stacks of $10,000 bundles from the bank" stuffed into large bags for delivery.

For some, though, Ross said that even that method of handoff was too risky. She claimed that Nygard got creative in his efforts to pay off the local politicos.

She recalled one particular instance that stank with corruption—literally.

"Mr. Nygard had required that I order some very large fish," she said in the interview recorded for this book. "He had about $100,000 in $10,000 bundles. He told me he wanted me to break them up, roll them, and put them in this fish."

Why the stinky secrecy? Ross claimed, "I'm assuming [the recipient] didn't want anybody to know he was receiving it."

"At the time he asked me to do it, I wasn't asking much questions," Ross explained. "I wanted to make sure my children were taken care of."

Still, the experience forever tainted her view of politics in her home nation. Ross said, "If the price is right, they don't think about anybody but themselves."

"It takes a mastermind to undermine that many people," she claimed. "Mr. Nygard strategically moved his way through the Bahamas."

According to records obtained by the *Bahamas Tribune*, Smith's former pal Shane Gibson (a member of the PLP) received $94,131.10 deposited directly into his Miami bank account from the Nygard Companies in 2012 and 2013. The donations were usually $5,000 or more, and were deposited on a semi-regular monthly basis, marked "services" or "travel."

When confronted with the records, Gibson, the Minister of Immigration and Labor at the time, told the *Tribune* that they were campaign donations, as well as financial contributions to community programs he was spearheading, like scholarships for local students. (Gibson would later be photographed grinning at one of Nygard's Bahamian "pamper parties" in 2014.)

Shane Gibson's brother, Eric, also was paid by the Nygard Companies throughout this period. A source for this book provided copies of checks made out to Eric Gibson totaling more than $100,000. The checks were all dated 2011 or 2012, and cut from the "Nygard Holdings Limited" account at the "Royal Bank of Canada Lyford Cay Shopping Center" branch. Some checks were as small as $500. Others were as large as $15,000.

Another tranche of check copies obtained for this book showed payments to one "Pat Smith," "believed to be an old PLP loyalist," according to one local report. Smith's checks were cut during the same period, and the grand total was nearly $40,000.

With Nygard's support, the PLP rolled to victory in 2012 and he was quick to claim credit. Nygard posted a video online titled "Nygard Takes Bahamas Back," which showed him celebrating the PLP win by popping bottles at Nygard Cay. Even more audacious was the clip he posted that showed him glad-handing various government ministers on the beach outside of his party palace.

Helpfully, Nygard gave each visitor their own chyron identifying their government position. Among the men who made the pilgrimage to Nygard Cay after the election were the following:

- Deputy Prime Minister, Phillip "Brave" Davis
- The Minister of Housing & National Insurance, Shane Gibson
- The Minister for Grand Bahamas, Dr. Michael Darville
- The Minister of Education, Jerome Gomez
- The Minister of Agriculture, V. Alred Gray
- The Minister of Housing & Environment, Ken Dorsett
- The Minister of Health, Dr. Perry Gomez
- The Director of Fertility, Dr. Wan Song

"It was the greatest victory we ever had!" Nygard bragged in the video, while the men around him laughed and sipped drinks.

Even Prime Minister Perry Christie was photographed at the property on September 5, 2012.

Community outrage was swift.

"Every one of them in that film, they all need to tender their resignations now," Loretta Butler-Turner, Deputy Director of the PLP's rival party, the FNM blasted. "Just seeing the way that they are with Mr. Nygard, it seems as though he feels that he is cozy with the government." Her sentiments were echoed by so many others.

Still, the members of the PLP were adamant that all donations had been above-board, and they were not giving Nygard any special treatment.

Minister of Agriculture V. Alfred Gray even gave an indignant speech outside of Bahamian Cabinet refuting the claims of cronyism.

"Mr. Nygard is a Bahamian, he is a philanthropist, and I think he has given more to this country than many other Bahamians," Gray said. "Including those who criticize him."

Insisting "the government is not for sale," Gray continued, "Mr. Nygard has done nothing wrong."

Even Nygard's critics had to admit that. One *Tribune* columnist wrote, "without any limits on what anyone can contribute and no campaign finance legislation to act as safeguards against buying the government you want, what Mr. Nygard did was perfectly legal."

"Nevertheless, whether the populace would have voted Christie and the PLP in 2012 without Mr. Nygard's $5 million is something we will never know," the columnist continued. "Just as we will never know how many $100 or $300 gifts were rolled up in T-shirts given out at PLP rallies prior to the election."

Nygard quickly cashed in on his favors.

According to court documents obtained by the *Tribune* newspaper, Nygard met with the new PLP Prime Minister's Senior Policy Advisor, Sir Baltron Bethel, just weeks after their election victory to discuss his plans to build a stem cell facility at Nygard Cay. Shortly thereafter, the government "determined that appropriate acreage should be leased to Mr. Peter Nygard" so he could rebuild Nygard Cay and develop a stem cell facility as a part of what was termed a "touristic development."

Nygard admitted to having had the meeting, but his attorneys later claimed that the minutes of that meeting had been fabricated, and that he had no desire to "curry preferential treatment by the Bahamian government."

The campaign to get his stem cell mecca built, though, would consume him for the next several years.

***

Nygard has always been obsessed with his appearance and virility. So when he discovered the power of stem cell treatments to reverse signs of aging, he was hooked. In the early 2000s, when the treatments were still very controversial,

Nygard became a stem cell crusader. In one YouTube video, he even compared himself to Ponce De Leon and his search for the fountain of youth. (The only difference? The video said, De Leon failed and Nygard found it.)

With his fashion lines thriving, Nygard launched "Nygard Biotech," and turned his efforts toward developing a massive stem cell facility. All he needed? The right country to host it. "We traveled everywhere in the world over the last two years just looking," he said in another YouTube video about his quest. He cut a deal in China to develop the technology, but decided that wasn't the right place to put down roots for his new project. "Owning the right technology would mean nothing without the appropriate country to embrace its use," the narrator of his YouTube video explained.

Perhaps unsurprisingly, Nygard decided that the Bahamas would get the honor of hosting the first-ever Nygard clinic. He insisted that it would be a boon for the country, and especially for its tourism industry. "This is basically like building a Mayo clinic," he bragged, insisting that it was only the first of many to come. The only problem? There was not yet any Bahamian legislation that would allow for stem cell treatments on the island. Good thing Nygard knew a few men in Parliament.

Nygard didn't wait long after the election to come collect from the prime minister, Perry Christie. Christie's medical adviser, Dr. Arthur Porter, described that early meeting in his book, *The Man Behind the Bow Tie*. He says that Nygard was annoyed, impatient, and ready to get his way.

"Normally relaxed, talkative and gregarious with a wide crinkly smile, at this moment the multi-millionaire fashion mogul was furious," Dr. Porter wrote. "Hot, flustered and impatient, he bounced an ankle on one knee, mumbling about broken promises."

Almost as soon as Christie entered the room, Dr. Porter wrote, Nygard exploded: "Do you intend on honoring our arrangement?!"

"The Prime Minister began to speak," he continued, "assuring him. Then adding the word but."

Nygard wasn't having it. Dr. Porter claimed he launched a tirade: "Before the election, we spoke about the stem cell bill being the first piece of legislation before the House of Assembly. Not the third. Not the second. The first. We are a week in, and I have heard nothing. You haven't taken my phone calls. I got a call back from one of your assistants."

Dr. Porter said that he had previously advised Christie "to go slowly and carefully with the stem cell legislation. It was too important to take a risk and get it wrong, and the Bahamas could be a leader in the field if it did it right."

Based on Nygard's behavior, Christie decided it couldn't wait.

The Prime Minister finally pushed the Stem Cell Therapy and Research Bill through Parliament in August 2013—and he made no secret of the fact that it had been inspired by Nygard. He said on the floor of Parliament in Nassau, "I want you to know that stem cell legislation will be passed by us today. God bless Peter Nygard!" In response, Nygard filmed a video for Christie's YouTube page, gushing, "Prime Minister Christie has shown historic leadership in passing this legislation."

However, he didn't let Christie take all the credit. In the video, Nygard said, "I initiated and helped to write the stem cell legislation I took that to many countries. Ultimately, the Bahamas adopted it into law." Bahamians were not happy with the implication that Nygard had given his wish list to Parliament and they had delivered, no questions asked.

In December 2013, the *Nassau Guardian* wrote that there were still lingering "questions about how involved fashion designer Peter Nygard was in the process, and whether the legislation was brought to appease him."

It was a line of inquiry that Nygard's political rivals happily encouraged. Leaders of the FNM party "later suggested that the government was pushing the bill as a pay back to Nygard," the paper reported, "an assertion the government denied."

When Nygard was asked point-blank about the role he had played in getting the legislation passed, he was coy despite his earlier boasts on YouTube. He said, "I don't know why anybody would paint that as doing it for me. I think [the Prime Minister] is doing it for the Bahamian people, for the Bahamas. . . . There's nothing in it for me."

That wasn't, however, what he was saying in private—especially as it became clear that the Bahamian government was taking the whole stem cell industry out of Nygard's hands. Politicians had established a regulatory ethics committee that would decide who could open stem cell businesses on the island. In effect, all of the power related to stem cells was out of the hands of Nygard's allies. He was furious.

Transcripts of Nygard's conversations from that period with his local henchmen "Tugi" and "Bobo" were entered into the court record and obtained for this book. They suggest that Nygard could barely contain his anger at the men he had thought he'd bought and paid for.

"We have a couple issues," he said in one summer 2015 conversation. "God damn, those guys didn't uphold their responsibilities."

"With a good damn committee, how embarrassing" he continued. "They dare to play paymasters and it's the Prime Ministers fault."

In another conversation, impatient Nygard grumbled, "There's no f***in reason it should take this long. [They] keep making these fake promises."

He'd had enough, and was ready to take his stem cell project to another country. "I'm not putting this shit here now," he told Tugi and Bobo. "I pissed away $5 million. Since the Prime Minister got me involved, it's cost me five f***in million dollars of bullshit."

The Bahamas continued to work through constructing their regulatory system, but Nygard took off for sunnier shores in St. Kitts—one thousand miles southeast of Grand Bahama. (Ironically, St. Kitts was just a short boat ride away from Jeffrey Epstein's "orgy island," Little St. James.)

In March 2015, Nygard was front and center at the St. Kitts Biomedical Research Foundation's Strategy Conference on Reverse Aging Treatments, alongside neurosurgeons and other leading scientists from the University of Pennsylvania, Yale, Harvard, and more. The two-day strategy session at the local Marriott "was attended by a dozen of the leading stem cell and experimental medicine experts from the United States," the local paper reported, "who reviewed numerous strategies that are being pursued around the world."

The paper noted that initial testing would need to be done on monkeys, and the island was notorious for having a rampant monkey population, which supplied the subjects for biomedical research at the St. Kitts Foundation.

For Nygard, it seemed like a perfect fit. At the group meeting, he announced a proposal to establish a stem cell health and wellness spa on the island's luxurious Christophe Harbour. The *St. Kitts-Nevis Times* reported that he hoped "to deliver some of these health-promoting and rejuvenating treatments to an international clientele."

The key to doing that, it was implied, would be a welcoming government. The paper explained, "The group discussed how the government can be supportive of these activities, while ensuring quality and safety of the treatments and how they should be regulated." It seemed that so far, the government was on board: Deputy Prime Minister Shawn Richards was spotted glad-handing attendees at the event.

Nygard hadn't given up on the Bahamas just yet, but he was hedging his bets and laying the groundwork in St. Kitts as his home island figured out how they would regulate the new industry. For perhaps the first time in the Bahamas, it seemed things wouldn't go his way.

In September 2016, the *International Medical Travel Journal* announced that the Bahamas had become the first English-speaking Caribbean nation to develop a regulatory framework for stem cell research and treatments. It wasn't the framework that Nygard had wanted.

Moving forward, the *Journal* reported, the National Stem Cell Ethics Committee would meet in January and June every year to review new applications. Operating an illegal clinic would result in a fine of $250,000, three to ten years in prison, or both.

"In theory, Nygard could still seek to set up his stem cell clinic," the *Journal* explained. "But the new stem cell rules mean that politicians have been taken out of the decision making process. So Nygard would have to convince the National Stem Cell Ethics Committee and its Miami advisor, that all is above board and legally sound."

It wasn't a task that he wanted to confront, and he wasn't willing to wait any longer. In early 2016, Nygard pushed forward with his St. Kitts project. Nygard was using his old Bahamas model, it seemed: Timothy Harris founded the PLP party for the first time in St. Kitts and was elected Prime Minister in 2015, amid rumors he'd received shady campaign donations.

In 2016, Prime Minister Harris and his Health Minister, Eugene Hamiltion, gave Nygard the go-ahead to take over three rooms at St. Kitts' Joseph N. France General Hospital to begin his stem cell research and treatment. In rushing it through, though, they neglected to tell the Chief Medical Officer, Dr. Patrick Martin. When he found out what was going on right under his nose, he was outraged.

Dr. Martin just happened to stumble upon the private ward one day, and was shocked to find that the doctors were not keeping medical records for the patients. Worse, they were not even licensed to practice in St. Kitts. One from Brazil, was sent packing immediately. Then so was Dr. Martin.

Almost immediately after making a fuss about Nygard's special project, Dr. Martin was ordered to go on vacation, which would be immediately followed by his mandated retirement. Still, he insisted he had no regrets about shutting Nygard's secret stem cell shop down. He told local radio station WINNFM, "Stem cell research or experimentation must be guided by ethical safeguards and other safeguards."

In another embarrassing blow for the government, one of Nygard's patients was named shortly after the scheme was revealed. The patient however, hadn't exactly planned to step forward.

Kentucky billionaire Richard Westin was stopped just before flying out of the Robert L. Bradshaw airport in St. Kitts—and was found to have a firearm in his luggage. Westin was charged with filing a false customs declaration, importation of a weapon, and failing to declare a weapon. He pleaded guilty to filing a false customs declaration and importation of a weapon, and paid a $10,000 fine. Locals called it "a slap on the wrist," and decried how instead of spending the night after his arrest in jail, Westin was shuttled to a local hotel.

(Strangely, a fact that was not discovered by reporters at the time is that shortly before Westin came to St. Kitts for his treatment, he was named the Title Secretary of an American nonprofit called the Nygard Stem Cell Genomic Foundation. The organization never reported any income or assets, and was quietly dissolved in 2017.)

In St. Kitts, local papers christened the debacle "The Stem Cell Scandal," and breathlessly reported on the mystery of what Nygard had been doing behind closed doors. The "In St. Kitts Nevis" news website, which calls itself "the premier information portal for St. Kitts and Nevis" even suggested that Nygard was using the placenta of new mothers at the hospital for his treatments—without their knowledge.

They weren't the only ones to make that outrageous claim. Nygard's former house manager, Richette Ross, said in an interview recorded for this book that Nygard "told me himself" about his stem cell harvesting.

Ross said that Nygard's chronically swollen knees seemed to have improved over time, and she asked what was behind the change. "He told me he used stem cells," she said. "Stem cells from the umbilical cord."

Umbilical cords were long thought of as prime harvesting material for stem cell researchers. A baby's cord has ten times more stem cells than can be found in other areas of the body, like bone marrow. What's more, stem cells from cord blood are less likely to carry infectious diseases, and also are half as likely to be rejected as stem cells harvested from an adult.

According to Ross, Nygard claimed he had found a way to improve even further on that material: She alleged that he said he had harvested umbilical cords from babies he had fathered. After getting a girlfriend pregnant, she said, "He told me he takes the girls to . . . abort the fetuses." (Umbilical cords form at just five weeks into a pregnancy.) Ross said Nygard claimed that since his own DNA was in the cord blood, it was a better "match."

One girl, Ross claimed, was even sent to China to have them harvest stem cells through her fetus. She claimed to have heard similar stories from other girls, too. "After they aborted," she said, "they told me they had just gotten back."

Nygard seemed to suggest that something like that could be afoot when he talked about the technology behind his treatments publicly. "I may be the only person in the world," he bragged, "who has my own embryos growing in a petri dish."

Suelyn Medeiros claims that she almost became Nygard's stem cell donor. In her 2014 memoir, she spins a bizarre and terrifying story. It all began out of the blue during a trip to Kiev, Ukraine. Nygard was having stem cell research done, and Medeiros was interested in biotechnology because her mother suffered from lupus.

"When he was finished, he said he had to talk to me about something," she writes. "He took me into a board meeting-type room with a large table surrounded by about 30 chairs. After we sat down, he asked, 'Suelyn, do you know what the best stem cells are?'"

She did: Embryos.

"Correct!" she says Nygard responded excitedly. "And you know what? If you got pregnant and had an abortion, we could use those embryonic cells and have a life's supply for all of us: you, your mother and me. A lot of people are doing it."

Nygard didn't seem to think it would be a hard sell, but Medeiros says she "was beyond stunned."

"This was the sickest thing I'd ever heard Peter say," she writes. "I thought he was going crazy. But looking back now, I realize that his obsession had taken him to a dark and very off-kilter place in his mind."

"I couldn't speak for a moment," she recalls. "Finally, catching my breath, I said, 'Peter I do not believe in abortion.'"

Nygard kept trying to convince her, she alleges, offering to compensate her "extremely well" if she were to move forward. Medeiros was disgusted, but she didn't know how she could say no.

"I spent my nights wrestling with whether I should do as he had asked, night after night after night, until I was consumed with angst and guilt," she writes.

"At first, I'd only been worried about our relationship: Could I keep it platonic? Could I continue to be his eye candy? But now there was much more at stake: my soul." Strangely, Nygard seemed to forget about his request after a while, and Medeiros was off the hook.

***

In just a few short years, Nygard's obsession with stem cells had destroyed the lives and careers of people around the world. Back in the Bahamas, Nygard's pal, Prime Minister Perry Christie, was under fire for his role in trying to push through Nygard's dream stem cell resort. In fact, his rivals used it as ammunition to get him out of power.

In 2013, former FNM chairman Darron Cash blasted the government over their close ties with Nygard. He said in a public statement, "Peter Nygard has taught the Christie government a valuable lesson. When the 'John' has finished paying for 'services' rendered, he feels as if he owns you. It is clear for all to see that the Prime Minister has gone out of his way to serve the needs and interests of this self-proclaimed paymaster."

"And now that Nygard has paid for political services rendered, he feels he can say or do anything he feels like in our country. Thank you for that, Prime Minister Christie!"

Still more disturbing details of Nygard's private meetings with high-ranking government officials emerged in the weeks prior to the 2017 general election. On May 5, 2017, *The Tribune* revealed details of a secret rendezvous in Las Vegas between Nygard, Shane Gibson, and Prime Minister Perry Christie.

The meetup had taken place shortly before the 2012 election, and was captured on video, according to court papers. The location "appeared to be a large hotel suite in the Palazzo Hotel in Las Vegas, whose signage is clearly reflected outside the window," the *Tribune* wrote.

Christie claimed it had all been aboveboard: "When I met with him, it wasn't Perry Christie and Nygard. It was Perry Christie, Nygard, and scientists from the University of California. And the matter wasn't what you could do for me, the matter was what can you do for the Bahamas."

Nygard later told friends that the meeting was actually evidence of how his PLP pals were beginning to turn on him. According to a source close to

Nygard, he called it "the height of humiliation" that the Prime Minister would only meet with him in another country. The source claimed that Nygard often complained about the PM dodging his calls.

Still, it was all too close to comfort for voters. In the May 2012 election, they ousted the PLP from power, replacing them with the FNM party. Nygard's direct line to the top of the Bahamian government was severed. If anything, the new administration had him in their sights, having run on the promise of ending the very type of corruption that he represented.

Perhaps not so coincidentally, Nygard fell into a spell of bad luck in his tropical paradise. Nygard Cay almost burned down due to an electrical fire in 2009, and that started a series of legal troubles that consumed him over the following years.

In September 2018, Nygard Cay was even seized by the Bahamian authorities over Nygard's failure to pay nearly $3 million in legal fees in one particular case. He paid a $2.6 million settlement in November 2018 to get the property back, but by January 2019 he was effectively banned from the country when a warrant was issued for his arrest. The problem? Nygard repeatedly failed to show up in court to face two contempt-of-court convictions. By all appearances, he hasn't returned since.

To friends, Nygard seemed disappointed that his donations didn't really end up paying off. He took advantage of a corrupt system without thinking about the fact that his targets might just as easily turn against him. It was a hard lesson to learn.

Soon, however, there would be even bigger legal troubles demanding Nygard's attention.

CHAPTER 8
HOLLYWOOD HELLHOUSE

I'm a builder of people. So when I see talent, I wanna just give it every opportunity to build that talent to the maximum.
—Peter Nygard

Scandals that would take any other businessman down seemed to barely dent the armor of Peter Nygard.

He handily waded through the explosion of sexual-harassment claims against him in the late 90s, and by the early 2000s, major international news headlines about Nygard mainly referred to his growing business. Until 2020.

On January 22, 2020, a former Nygard employee named Maridel Carbuccia filed an explosive lawsuit against Nygard and his associated companies in L.A. What she had to say was as familiar for followers of Nygard as it was disturbing. She then filed an amended complaint on January 31, taking on famed victims' rights attorney Gloria Allred as her lawyer.

According to Carbuccia, she was living in Florida in 2015 when she met Nygard through a mutual friend. She had recently resigned from her job of thirteen years as a corporate treasurer in order to care for her son, who was suffering from seizures.

At their first meeting, Nygard divulged that he was branching out from the clothing business to open a medical marijuana facility in California. According to Carbuccia's filing, he was "concerned that his then-business partner was misappropriating funds from the" project.

Nygard was impressed by Carbuccia's corporate background, among other things. He suggested she join his company as a "Treasurer/Controller/ Project Manager," tasked with making "sure that the funds he was investing in the project were properly accounted for," states the suit.

Carbuccia was intrigued—especially because medical marijuana was not then legal in Florida, and she wondered if it could help ease her son's medical issues. She flew with Nygard on his private jet to Los Angeles in November 2015, and toured the site. Impressed, she agreed to work with him on a temporary basis as they finalized the details of her position.

Carbuccia was excited about her new opportunity. It almost seemed too good to be true. According to Carbuccia, it was.

One day, out of nowhere, she claims that Nygard finally showed his true colors. According to the lawsuit, Nygard, "who had not previously acted in a sexual manner" toward Carbuccia, "unexpectedly grabbed her buttocks."

Carbuccia could hardly believe it. "She was shocked and upset and made those feelings clearly known to Nygard," the lawsuit states. "He immediately apologized to her and said that such things would not happen again."

"Nygard's apology appeared sincere," according to the lawsuit and Carbuccia "was willing to move on." More than that, she was willing to discuss making their arrangement more permanent. She wouldn't rely on the kind of oral agreement that had spelled doom for Nancy Ebker.

In early March 2016, Carbuccia and Nygard put together a written job agreement. Included as an exhibit in the lawsuit, the terms included the following:

- Carbuccia would move her family from Florida to LA
- She would receive a salary of $120,000 per year
- Car allowance of $40,000
- Moving expenses of $30,000
- Rent subsidy of $5,000 per month for two years
- A 5 percent equity stake in the medical marijuana project

Obviously, "Nygard did not disclose any intention (1) to condition her employment upon being subjected to sexual contact with him, or (2) to require that she facilitate his sexual encounters with apparent prostitutes as part of her employment," the lawsuit claims. Now, however, Carbuccia believes "he had no intention" of giving her what her job offer promised. In fact, according to the lawsuit, she believes he hired her and moved her to California with the express intent to make her prey to his sexual harassment.

With the job agreement secured, Carbuccia's lawsuit claims that Nygard didn't wait long before unleashing his inner monster:

One day in April 2016, the lawsuit claims, Carbuccia was going about her daily duties in Nygard's Marina Del Rey home when suddenly, "Nygard emerged from his room into the area where the plaintiff was waiting for him. To her horror, she saw that he was completely naked."

According to the lawsuit, it wasn't a mistake; the situation quickly got even worse.

"As he came toward the plaintiff," the complaint claims, "he said, 'Nothing is free in this world.'"

Carbuccia "was very upset by what she saw and heard, and left the third floor of Nygard's residence." She hoped she'd made her feelings clear with her departure, and gave her boss some time to get dressed while she cooled off.

Later, when she returned to work, "Nygard was present and was not acting suspiciously," the lawsuit states. "At one point, Nygard provided the plaintiff with a drink."

With her guard down and trusting her new boss, Carbuccia consumed it.

"After consuming the drink Nygard offered her that day, the plaintiff began to pass out," the lawsuit states. "She recalls, however, that as she began to pass out, Nygard led her to his bedroom."

"The next morning when she awoke, she saw her own blood on her skin and clothes, and it was apparent that while she was unconscious, Nygard had sexually assaulted her."

Stunned, Carbuccia "was too ashamed to reveal what had been done to her" and felt trapped because her wages were supporting her family, the lawsuit claimed. She had already begun the process of moving them across the country from Florida to LA. She decided to bite the bullet and stay on the job, unaware that things could get a whole lot worse.

In July 2016, Nygard's LA house manager went on a leave of absence. According to Carbuccia, Nygard implied that keeping her job would require taking on that house manager's duties.

Far beyond the duties of a trained financial professional like Carbuccia, those duties would include "inviting women to attend gatherings that Nygard called 'pamper parties,'" the lawsuit alleges. "The women who were invited to Nygard's 'pamper parties' included prostitutes, and the parties enable Nygard to to get a good look at them, and to select those whom he would pay for sex."

Carbuccia claims that Nygard often gave her lists of women to invite to the parties, and even had her check them in at the door. Everyone was required to sign a confidentiality agreement, she says. To Carbuccia, it was clear what was going on.

All throughout this period, Carbuccia "was aware that selected women spent the night for sexual purposes and that Nygard paid the women for their sexual services," the lawsuit claims.

Carbuccia was not happy. "Among other things, she told him that she was not a madam, and that she did not want to be involved in such activities," the complaint states. According to Carbuccia, Nygard made it clear that she had to continue with those tasks, or she would be fired.

At the same time, Carbuccia says, Nygard was making her life a living hell in so many other ways. "Continuing through December of 2016," the lawsuit states, Nygard "grabbed" her "buttocks on numerous occasions without her consent, in a manner that was highly offensive to her, and for sexual gratification. He disregarded her protests." Worse, she claims, he failed to pay her the salary and incentives that were part of her original job offer.

For all of these reasons, Carbuccia's lawsuit explains, she decided that her work environment with Nygard was truly "intolerable," and she resigned in

December 2016. She had no idea what her family would do to survive, but in her mind anything was better than spending her days in Nygard's hellhouse.

Nygard wasn't letting her go so easily. Carbuccia claims that he launched an all-out campaign to win her back, insisting that "he would no longer act in a sexual manner toward her, and that she would no longer be required to act as his house manager."

The lawsuit alleges, "He also said that her resignation had been a kind of wake up call to him."

It was all very believable. Carbuccia finally caved, and went to a February 2017 meeting at his home to talk about coming back to work. What she found there was not the usual Nygard.

"He was wearing an adult diaper and he appeared pale," the lawsuit claims. "He explained that he had recently undergone surgery, and asked her to excuse his appearance."

"During the same meeting, Nygard implied that he was no longer sexually active, apologized for his prior sexual batteries upon [Carbuccia]," and "stated unequivocally that he would never again" touch her in a sexual manner, the lawsuit claims.

He also renewed his promise to pay her $120,000 a year, plus a car allowance of $40,000, reimbursed moving expenses of $30,000, a rental allowance of $5,000 per month for two years, health and dental insurance, and a 5 percent stake in his cannabis project.

Carbuccia was "in a desperate financial situation because of her unemployment" and his failure to keep his earlier promises, the lawsuit alleges. More importantly, it appeared to Carbuccia that Nygard was "serious about reforming his ways." She agreed to give him a second chance—a decision that she would later regret.

Not long after her second run of work for Nygard began, the lawsuit claims, the Finnish fashion designer once again resumed "subjecting her to sexual batteries and assaults." Grabbing her buttocks became a common occurrence, according to the lawsuit, but everything reached a whole new level on January 22, 2018.

The complaint states that on that date, Nygard scheduled a business meeting with Carbuccia—who was pregnant at the time. It quickly went south, to say the least.

Partway through the conversation, the complaint states, "Nygard suddenly reached out" and grabbed Carbuccia's breasts. "As he did that he remarked that her 'ass' looked 'amazing' and then asked, 'You know what they say about pregnant women?' Answering his own question, Nygard said, 'They want it more' while making sexual motions with his hips."

All in all, Carbuccia found it "extremely upsetting" and "offensive." Soon after that meeting, she would miscarry her unborn child.

Like so many of the women before her, Carbuccia held on to her employment at Nygard so she could pick up the paycheck that would support her family. Despite the alleged assaults she persevered and tried to do her job. Ultimately, it would be Nygard himself who booted her out in 2018, after she raised concerns about how he was operating his medical marijuana facility.

It was three strange years that Carbuccia would never get back—and from which, she claims, she might never recover. According to her attorneys, she "has suffered and will continue to suffer pain and suffering, severe mental anguish and emotional distress, and economic damages" from Nygard's "intentional and outrageous" behavior. Now, she wants him to pay.

At press time, Nygard had not filed a response to her complaint, but a court date was set for June 2020.

Although it was filed in Los Angeles, the case was not picked up by the local papers. It would be weeks before anyone would really notice that it had been filed. All in all, the Carbuccia lawsuit was initially more of a quiet ripple than a splash. But the tsunami was on its way.

CHAPTER 9
HAVING THEIR SAY

The philosophy is, "What's good for me is good for everybody, right?"
—Peter Nygard

It could have been a sort of early Valentine's Day gift from the many women who had been crossed by Peter Nygard over the years: a ninety-nine-page class action complaint unleashed in New York on February 13, 2020, accusing Nygard of "rape," "sexual assault," sex trafficking," sodomy, corruption, and so much more. Like never before, women from the United States, the Bahamas, and other countries around the world had united to sue Peter Nygard, Nygard Inc., Nygard International Partnership, and Nygard Holdings Limited in the US District Court for the Southern District of New York.

Their claims included the following:

1. Violation of the Trafficking Victim Protection Act
2. Participating in a venture in violation of The Trafficking Victim Protection Act
3. Conspiracy to commit violation of the Trafficking Victim Protection Act

Their demand? A jury trial, damages, and legal fees. Even more, they were demanding to be heard at last.

The complaint was blistering from the start. According to the women's attorneys, Nygard "recruited, lured and enticed young, impressionable, and often impoverished children and women, with cash payments and false promises of lucrative modeling opportunities to assault, rape, and sodomize them."

"Nygard used his considerable influence in the fashion industry, his power through corruption of officials, and a network of company employees under his direction, to groom and entice underage girls and women," the complaint alleges.

According to the lawsuit, the promise of a modeling career wasn't all that Nygard used to ensnare these women in his web, however: When required, Nygard would use "alcohol, drugs, force, fraud, and/or other forms of coercion" to rape the children and women unlucky enough to cross his path.

He wasn't the only one to blame. The lawsuit specifically targeted his companies—which had recently passed annual sales of $500 million—because allegedly, the very companies were as guilty as their namesake himself.

The complaint claims that the companies "were instrumental knowingly aiding, abetting, facilitating, and participating in Nygards' decades-long sex-trafficking scheme," by funding his "sex trafficking" scheme, recruiting his victims, and paying them off to keep their silence about what they endured. In excruciating detail, the lawsuit lays out the many ways that Nygard's corporate funds and corporate employees became enmeshed in his extracurricular activities. From data entry that included full-body photographs, to event planning that required a guest list of teens, Nygard employees had unwittingly enabled so much horror to be perpetrated upon young girls and women around the world.

Says the lawsuit, "The destruction of innocent lives is immeasurable."

***

Allegedly, Nygard had his whole web of international sexual assault down to a science. Over the years, he had crafted the perfect trap for his prey, a sick system known as the "pamper parties."

Nygard hosted the infamous events at Nygard Cay and at his home in Marina del Rey, California, on a weekly basis (usually on Sundays) when he was in town.

What exactly happened at a pamper party? "On the surface, young girls and women are invited to enjoy the amenities of Nygard Cay and are pampered for the day with free photo shoots, manicures, pedicures and massages," the lawsuit explained. The parties were frequently promoted on social media, and women from the Bahamas, United States, and the wider Caribbean often attended. Nygard even promoted the parties on his corporate accounts, perhaps as some kind of branding move that was meant to show his appreciation for his female customers.

What happened behind the scenes, however, would have shocked and horrified the middle-aged moms buying his polyester pants at the local department store.

The real purpose of the pamper parties, according to the class action suit, was to bring women to Nygard Cay so that Nygard could then rape them. The claim alleges that staffers from an entire department of his company—the Corporate Communications Coordinators—were tasked with stocking his parties with potential victims. Whether meeting them on the street, at the mall, or on Facebook, the employees would invite pretty young girls and women to come check out the scene, the suit says, and their lives would never be the same. Here's how it all went down, according to the suit:

> Nygard's Corporate Communications Coordinators (ComCor) . . . were used to ensure that Nygard's potential victims attended the "pamper parties" by contacting them and arranging for their transportation to the parties.
>
> Upon arrival at the gated Nygard Cay property, most of Nygard's victims were required to "register" with ComCor, which was in charge of planning and coordinating corporate events, by providing their personal information, such as their names, telephone numbers, email addresses, and the identities of the persons who invited them.
>
> They were also required to pose for headshots and full-body photographs. The pictures and registration forms, filled out by the

Nygard employees, were scanned and emailed directly to Nygard, so that he could review who was in attendance, while sitting upstairs in his bedroom. Nygard would then use this information to select his potential victims for the night.

What was Nygard's selection criteria? According to the lawsuit, he demanded "an eight in the face, and a nice toilet," or rear end.

"The information was then entered into a company database, so that Nygard had a ready list of 'prospective recruits' who were potential victims to pursue at any given time."

Nygard's database dated back to 1987, according to an inside source, and featured more than seven thousand girls and young women. Shockingly, he didn't do much to keep it a secret. The database was hosted on the corporate server, and maintained by the company's IT department. (Nygard's longtime head of IT, Daane Thomas, died suddenly only a few months before the New York lawsuit was filed, at the age of forty-four. A source close to the family told me that the timing of his death was a tragic coincidence, and foul play was not suspected.)

Internal Nygard company documents filed with the lawsuit suggest that ComCor employees were completely aware of what their dirty database was intended to achieve. In one messaging exchange filed with the court, an employee brags, "all a dem" girls that were in the Cay that night "wan fuck." The other person asks if it wasn't "too much pussy for one night? :o" The employee responded, "Everyone he's interested in he's slept with before and they can't make it." The employee continued to explain how she was desperately trying to get a new girl to commit to coming, but had encountered resistance so far.

For those that did accept the invitation, it was always a once-in-a-lifetime experience—for better or for worse. After registering at the door, they would be ushered into the overwhelming grounds of Nygard Cay, a place that was both fantasyland and hellscape.

"Once they enter the property, no one at Nygard Cay is allowed to leave the property without Nygard's express permission," the lawsuit claimed.

"The security gate staff will not open the gate, unless they are instructed to do so by Nygard himself. . . . The only way out, other than the main gate, is to swim through shark-infested waters." Bahamian locals claim that according to urban legend, some women had tried to do just that.

At the beginning, though, most guests probably just felt lucky to experience the life of an A-lister. Getting a manicure or a massage—often for the first time in their lives—they had no idea what was in store. As the women blithely went about their pampering, the lawsuit alleged, Nygard would have already crafted his plan of attack.

"Nygard has a preference for young girls and prefers underaged victims. After he selects his victims for the night, Nygard either himself or through his groomers, encourages the children and young women to drink wine, 'happy juice,' or other alcoholic beverages," the court documents claim. "If the young girls or women are resistant, he sometimes has his bartenders lace the victims' drinks with drugs such as Rohypnol (roofies)."

On so many nights, it was alleged, the same story would unfold:

> Nygard then lures the victims to his bedroom or has them ushered there by groomers, under the false pretense of discussing a potential modeling contract in private, where he uses physical force or coercion or knowing the victim has not attained the age of 18 years, to engage in commercial sex acts and coerce and force them to engage in unwanted sexual acts . . .
>
> Nygard's personal security guard often stands outside the door to his bedroom, so that nobody can enter and so that his victims cannot leave. After each encounter, the victim cannot leave without Nygard's personal permission, further extending the victim's horror and humiliation.
>
> The amounts of money provided to the victims is more than most of his victims have seen at one time in their entire lifetimes. In addition to US currency, Nygard promises this money is just a start to what he can provide for the victims. He promises many

victims that he will contact them about future modeling contracts.

However, in the vast majority of cases, Nygard never intends to follow through with the modeling contracts and tells his victims this for the sole purpose of maintaining control over them. If he does provide any modeling opportunities, it is for the purpose of compelling additional sex acts.

Nygard also threatens the victims with implied or express threats of retribution if they tell anyone about what happened, often implying or expressly threatening to have his victims killed if they do not cooperate.

Women who were brought in from other countries could have faced another level of horror. According to the lawsuit, "When girls would be flown into the Bahamas on the N-Force jet for 'pamper parties,' the passengers would have their passports collected, their return flight was cancelled by the travel agency personnel, and approval from Nygard was required to leave Nygard Cay and the island. Nygard expected a sex act before he was willing to consider releasing any person."

Even in cool legalese, the allegations are disturbing. Far more chilling than the straightforward allegations about his sex-trafficking scheme, however, are the stories of the ten women who claim they were its victims. Please be warned: Their allegations are incredibly graphic and heartbreaking.

JANE DOE 1

Age when she was allegedly raped by Nygard: Fourteen

On the 4th of July in 2001, Jane Doe 1 was hanging out at the local Bahamian mall with friends. The Nygard Store had recently opened there, and promotional models were walking throughout the mall, chatting up shoppers to create a buzz.

When Jane Doe 1 walked by the Nygard store, the lawsuit claims, "a model was standing in the entrance and asked her to come inside. The model handed her a pair of pants and told her to try them on."

Jane Doe 1 "went to the changing room, but the changing room had no curtains or doors on them. As she began to change, three of the workers began taking pictures," the lawsuit states. "She asked if there was anywhere else to change, and the models responded that the rooms were still being renovated, and there was nowhere else to go."

In the midst of that humiliating moment, Peter Nygard suddenly swept into the room. Noticing that her pants were too big, he asked to take her measurements—and began rubbing "her inner thighs and buttocks" in the process.

While he went to work, Nygard asked Jane Doe 1 what grade she was in, the lawsuit states, and she "responded that she was in Grade 9." Next, Nygard asked her if she had ever modeled, allegedly telling the naive fourteen-year-old "that she had the body for it."

"Nygard told her that his name was Peter Nygard and asked her if she wanted to work for him," the suit continues. "Nygard instructed her to give one of the models her phone number," and Jane Doe 1 did, "because she wanted to be a model."

In just a few days, she got a call from one of Nygard's employees, asking her to come to Nygard's home to discuss her modeling dreams. She was told to be ready at 6:00 p.m., in a dress, heels, and makeup, and that everything else would unfold from there.

At the appointed time, the lawsuit says, Jane Doe 1 "was picked up in a white SUV at her house by another Nygard employee. When she got in the car, there were already two girls in the back seat."

"When they arrived at Nygard Cay, the three girls were registered at the security office and subsequently escorted to a dining area near the beach. They ate with other guests while they waited for Nygard to join them. Nygard eventually joined them and began playing poker."

Still uneasy about what she had gotten herself into, Jane Doe 1 was reassured when Nygard finally pulled her aside and asked if she was ready to "discuss business." Nygard led her upstairs, the lawsuit claims, and she was still under the impression that they were about to negotiate her future. When they entered a bedroom instead of an office, though, the lawsuit says she became "nervous."

According to the court documents, "Nygard assured her that he doesn't bite and told her to sit down and get comfortable. Nygard then turned on the television, which immediately began showing pornography . . . of a man rubbing feces over a woman's body."

"Nygard then went into a closet that was next to the bed and pulled out a dildo and K-Y Jelly. Nygard asked her to 'try something new.'"

Jane Doe 1 "responded that she could not do that and that she only came to discuss modeling," the documents state. "Nygard responded that he would discuss modeling afterwards. He instructed Jane Doe No. 1 to pick up the dildo, apply the K-Y Jelly, and to insert it into his anus."

The allegations filed in court continue:

> Nygard got onto the bed and knelt down on his knees, turning and pointing his anus towards her.
>
> Nygard repeated his instructions, but with more force.
>
> Jane Doe No. 1 did as she was instructed because she was afraid.
>
> Over her objections, Nygard used force and fear to have her penetrate his anus with a lubricated dildo, while he masturbated.
>
> Nygard then told Jane Doe No. 1 that it was her turn to "have some fun." Nygard approached her and she asked him to stop. Nygard, ignoring her rejection, reached around her neck, began unzipping her dress, put on a condom, kissed her, and began to open her legs.
>
> As she tried to close her legs and push him off of her, he held her hands back and pinned them against the headboard. The victim, a virgin, cried as Nygard forced his penis into her vagina, causing extraordinary trauma and pain.

For Nygard, the lawsuit claims, it was all over as quickly as it had begun. He instructed Jane Doe 1 to go into the bathroom and put her clothes on. The suit claims, "her makeup was messy from crying. She cleaned her face and went back into the bedroom, at which point Nygard told her it was time to go."

On the way out, he allegedly gave her an envelope—filled with cash.

Stunned, Jane Doe 1 went back to the dining area, where she found the two Nygard employees who brought her there. A Nygard employee escorted her to a car and transported her back home.

"She never told anyone what happened to her because she was afraid and embarrassed," the suit says. "She never returned to Nygard Cay."

JANE DOE 2

Age when allegedly raped by Nygard: Fourteen

In 2011, at the age of fourteen, Jane Doe 2 entered the Miss Teen Bahamas Galaxy beauty pageant competition in the hopes of launching an international modeling career.

"Her family was impoverished, and they sought sponsorship to help her cover her pageant costs," the lawsuit states. A family friend "suggested that she contact Nygard as he might be interested," so the girl's mother compiled a portfolio of photos and sent it off to Nygard Cay.

Nygard was known in the Nassau area for supporting local charities, and especially ones benefiting underprivileged children.

At first, however, it seemed like Jane Doe 2 would not be so lucky. An employee quickly responded that Nygard "was not granting scholarships at that time." The girl's mother persisted, and "eventually she developed a relationship with Nygard's daughter, Bianca Nygard," the lawsuit claims. Bianca was a frequent fixture at Nygard Cay, and throughout the local community. She quickly struck up a rapport with Jane Doe 2 and her mom.

In June, the mother-daughter duo were finally invited to visit Nygard Cay during a pamper party. Everything appeared to be aboveboard, and the mother-daughter duo simply enjoyed their day. As they were leaving, the suit states, Bianca told them to resubmit the photos. This time, the images of the fourteen-year-old caught Nygard's eye.

Jane Doe 2 and her mother were invited back for another pamper party in August 2011. At the gate, however, a security guard told the girl's mother "that she did not need to attend the pamper party" with her fourteen-year-old daughter, the lawsuit states.

According to the court documents, the guard claimed that the girl "was like family now" and would be protected inside the Nygard Cay gates. The mom was skeptical. She insisted on staying, and they both got pedicures before heading home as planned.

Two weeks later however, Nygard employees allegedly bypassed Jane Doe 2's mother, sending her a personal invite to another pamper party through her WhatsApp directly. This time, she didn't tell her mom, out of fear that she'd say she couldn't go.

"When she arrived, there were a number of young girls her age, including another pageant contestant who she knew," the lawsuit states, which made her feel less uncertain about her decision. She got a manicure and was exploring the grounds when she saw Nygard at a table with a group of girls.

"She did not approach Nygard, but noticed him looking at her," the lawsuit claims, and soon, Nygard's driver approached to take her over to "the boss."

Jane Doe 2 "responded that she did not feel comfortable going over to talk to Nygard," the court documents claim, but "the driver told her that if she went over to talk with him, Nygard would give her a sponsorship" for her beauty pageant.

Could it be her big break? Jane Doe 2 swallowed her fear and made her way over to the fashion mogul, surely with dreams of sequins and crystal crowns in her head. Immediately, she claims, Nygard seemed impressed.

According to the court documents, he "told her that she was beautiful and that she had 'luscious lips.'"

More than ever, her pageant dreams seemed in reach as Nygard went out of his way to make her feel comfortable.

"Nygard asked Jane Doe No. 2 what she was drinking, and she responded that she was drinking cranberry juice," the lawsuit claims. "Nygard asked her if she drank alcohol and she responded that she was a teenager and was not allowed to drink. Nygard told her that she was at a private event and could do whatever she wanted. . . . Nygard then instructed the bartender to bring her a glass of red wine."

He turned on the charm, and launched into a typical spiel.

Nygard "told her that if she stuck with him, she could travel all over the world with him," the lawsuit alleges. "He pointed to several other women in the room who were models and traveled with him to fashion shows in New York and London."

The drinks, she says, kept coming. Throughout the course of that conversation, the fourteen-year-old downed at least four glasses of wine. Eventually, she says, Nygard called the bartender over and whispered in his ear.

"The bartender returned with a bag of pills," the lawsuit claims. "There were white, blue, and pink pills all in a small blue ziplocked bag. Nygard showed the bag to Jane Doe No. 2 and told her that the pills would help her become a model, because all models did them. He told her that the pills would make her feel good and help her do well."

She believed him. Jane Doe 2 downed the pills, and roughly fifteen minutes later, "she began to feel dizzy, and the room began to spin," she claims. "She returned to the table where another glass of wine was waiting for her." Things were getting out of hand.

"Nygard then escorted her away from the foyer area, holding her hand, and led her to his bedroom," the lawsuit continues. "Once they arrived in his bedroom, Nygard laid her down on the bed and told her to relax."

"He walked away for approximately five minutes and returned with a dildo in his hands," the suit alleges. "Nygard removed her pants and underwear and attempted to force a dildo into her vagina. She resisted and told him to stop because it hurt. But Nygard did not stop; instead, he instructed her to 'relax' and stated that 'it has to be done sooner or later.' At that point, she blacked out and does not know what Nygard did to her while she was unconscious."

"The next morning, she woke and saw Nygard still sleeping next to her in the bed. She immediately got out of bed and noticed blood on the sheets. She went to the bathroom and immediately cleaned herself up. There was blood around her vagina."

According to the lawsuit, Nygard instructed Jane Doe 2 not to tell anyone what happened and told her that he would look out for her future as he handed her $5,000 in US currency.

Quickly, Jane Doe 2 "was escorted to a black bus that had a picture of Nygard's face on it. She was the only person on the bus, and the driver took her" to a mall, she says, where her aunt picked her up. She had been a virgin before that night.

Three months went by before Jane Doe 2 got an invitation to another pamper party via text. Despite what had happened the last time, she decided to go, the lawsuit explains, "because she believed that Nygard would make her a model—like he had promised he would do." She still had a shred of hope that her sacrifice would be worth it.

Sadly, she claims her night would unfold in much the same way as it had the last time.

As soon as Jane Doe 2 arrived, the lawsuit alleges, Nygard was back on the attack.

"Nygard approached her and asked her how she was doing," the lawsuit claims. "He began instructing the bartender to bring her wine again. He again offered her pills," but this time she declined.

Nygard again took her to his bedroom, the lawsuit alleges, where he "instructed" her to "play with his genitals, gave her lubricant and a dildo, and told her to penetrate his anus. Afraid, and hoping for the modeling opportunity that Nygard had promised," she did it.

That decision would change her life forever. Desperate to feel like it had all been worth it, Jane Doe 2 became a "regular guest" at Nygard Cay, "on the hope that she would become an international model for the Nygard brand."

For the next several years, there was no sign of that happening. When she finally did get her big break thanks to Nygard, it was hardly a glamorous international debut: In 2015, Nygard launched his Nygard Slims brand at the local mall, and Jane Doe 2 was hired to model pants. She was given a check for more than $3,000 from the Nygard Companies for her service, and a promotion—but not the one she was hoping for.

Instead of sending Jane Doe 2 off to strut the world's catwalks, Nygard "converted her into a recruiter to secure other young girls for him to abuse."

More hopeless than ever, she did it, the lawsuit states, "so that she would not have to satisfy his perverse sexual desires herself."

This, the lawsuit explains, was the darkest period of her life. Allegedly, Nygard would even "instruct her to offer the young girls drugs. . . . If the girls did not want to sleep with Nygard, Jane Doe No. 2 would sometimes put the drugs in their drinks or food without their knowledge."

Each time that she visited Nygard Cay and recruited girls for him, Nygard allegedly gave Jane Doe 2 a large sum of cash—never less than $2,000 and always in US currency.

The cycle of horror escalated to a whole new level during a pamper party at Nygard Cay on February 7, 2017, when Nygard allegedly pulled Jane Doe 2 back into sexual servitude.

On that date, the lawsuit alleges, "Nygard insisted that she defecate and/ or urinate in his mouth. She responded that she did not wish to do that to him. He offered to give her drugs that would help her defecate. She told Nygard no and decided that she could no longer take Nygard's perverse sexual fetishes."

That was the last straw. She left, and never returned again.

JANE DOES 3 & 4

Ages when allegedly raped by Nygard: Fourteen and Fifteen

Jane Does 3 and 4 were cousins who lived in an underprivileged neighbor-hood outside of Nassau. Their stories show how easily young women were brought into his web—and how the silence of sexual assault victims can ultimately sentence so many other women to the same fate.

In June 2011, Jane Doe 3 was hanging out with girlfriends in her neigh-borhood when one of Nygard's employees approached the group.

"She stated that she had a job for them to do, but did not specify what the job was," the lawsuit says. Jane Doe 3 was interested.

"The next day, at approximately 1:00 p.m., a white SUV arrived at Jane Doe No. 3's house and transported her to Nygard Cay. When she arrived, she saw the employee who told her that the job was not ready yet, and to go to the salon until she returned."

Jane Doe 3 treated herself to a massage—the first she'd ever had in her life—and sat down to eat and chat with some of the other girls. While she was enjoying herself under the Bahamian sun, the employee returned, "and told her that she wanted her to meet someone."

Still assuming she was there for a job interview, Jane Doe 3 "followed her upstairs to Nygard's bedroom, where she was introduced to Nygard, who was sitting at a small round table," the lawsuit claims. They began chatting, and the employee left the room. The lawsuit continues:

He offered her two glasses of wine, which she accepted. Nygard asked her if she had sex before; she said no. At this point, she became afraid.

Nygard sat her on the bed and began to rub her legs and face. He sat down next to her and slowly pushed her body back onto the bed. Nygard took a condom from the drawer and put it on.

He began kissing her on her stomach; she began trembling in fear. She shouted "no" and began to cry. Nygard grabbed her closer, put all of his weight on her, and penetrated her vagina with his penis. She told him to stop and resisted him, but he overpowered her.

After Nygard ceased vaginally raping her, she was bleeding from her vagina. There was also blood on the sheets. Jane Doe No. 3 told Nygard that she wanted to go. He pointed her to the bathroom and told her to clean off. She took a shower, and when she finished, Nygard was no longer in the room. She got dressed and waited for someone to return.

Eventually, the employee returned and asked her if she was okay. She responded that she was afraid. The employee led her back downstairs.

Jane Doe 3 sat quietly by herself until her driver returned, and on her way out, the employee who had invited her gave her $200.

The next week, the neighborhood girls were chattering again about yet another Sunday pamper party that was happening at Nygard Cay. Jane Doe 3 bragged to her fourteen-year-old cousin, Jane Doe 4, about the employee's job offer and the fun things she had seen there. She did not, however, tell her friends or cousin the full extent of what she had allegedly experienced. Instead, she agreed to go with them to Nygard Cay yet again.

When the group arrived, Jane Doe 3 became overwhelmed and told her friends she was not feeling well. She sat down alone, while they went off to explore and eat. Before long, Jane Doe 3 had lost track of her young cousin.

"She asked one of the other girls at the pamper party where she went, and they told her that she went with the employee" that had invited them, the lawsuit states.

As Jane Doe 3 frantically searched for her cousin, another party guest told her "that her mother was outside the gate at Nygard Cay, threatening to call the police if they did not let her in to get the girls," the lawsuit claims. "She did not want to leave without Jane Doe No. 4, and she was very scared." She should have been.

Meanwhile, across the compound, Jane Doe 3's cousin had changed into her bathing suit and picked up an alcoholic drink.

She was enjoying the night when Nygard "approached her and asked her if she had ever thought about modeling," the lawsuit claims. "He told her that he thought that she would be a good candidate, based on her body structure. He then told her that he had connections, if she wanted to try it."

The lawsuit continues:

Nygard asked her if she wanted to go somewhere and talk and motioned for her to follow him. He led her up the stairs, at which point Jane Doe No. 4 began to hesitate. He told her not to be scared.

She followed him up the stairs and into his bedroom. Once they arrived in the bedroom, Nygard invited her to get comfortable on the bed. Nygard turned on the television, which was playing pornography showing a woman having oral sex with a man.

After some time, Nygard sat down on the bed next to her and began stroking her hair and rubbing her back. Jane Doe No. 4 was scared and uncomfortable.

She asked him if this was his way of talking about modeling, and he replied that he wanted to have sex with her. Nygard began removing his clothes and moved toward her. Nygard pulled the strings on her bathing suit, removing it, and began licking her neck, moving downward until he began performing oral sex on her.

Jane Doe No. 4 attempted to close her legs, but Nygard pushed them open. She continued to try to close her legs, but he overpowered her. Nygard then moved upward and began to penetrate her vagina with his penis. After some time, he then instructed her to perform oral sex on him until he ejaculated. Prior to this encounter, she was a virgin.

As Nygard ushered Jane Doe 4 out, the lawsuit claims, he gave her an envelope with $5,600 and told her to leave her contact information with his team so that he could contact her about modeling.

"As she was heading downstairs, she saw her cousin, Jane Doe No. 3, looking for her and saying that her mother was outside waiting for them," the lawsuit claims. They left, neither talking about what had happened. She never returned to Nygard Cay.

JANE DOE 5

Age when allegedly raped by Nygard: Sixteen

Like so many other young Bahamian girls, Jane Doe 5 first heard about the infamous pamper parties through a teen friend, who offered to bring her along for free massages and manicures. Jane Doe 5 was excited to finally check it out.

As they explored the grounds, Jane Doe 5 "consumed multiple alcoholic beverages," the lawsuit states. While she and her friend were drinking on the beach, Nygard appeared, gesturing to her friend "to follow him."

Jane Doe 5's friend motioned for her to come along, "because she did not want to go with Nygard alone," the lawsuit claims. "Nygard took them up to his bedroom and gave them more to drink."

Before long, "Jane Doe No. 5 began to feel very 'loose,'" the lawsuit alleges. "Nygard instructed the girls to touch one another sexually, and they complied. After several minutes, Nygard joined and began touching the girls."

Then, the lawsuit claims, he pushed the boundaries even further: "During the encounter, Nygard sodomized Jane Doe No. 5 against her will. Afterwards, she was bleeding from her anus. Nygard then asked the girls to defecate on him, but neither of them could or would do so."

That ended it. Nygard allegedly gave Jane Doe 5 $200 and dismissed her. She could finally say she had been to a party at Nygard Cay. She never returned.

JANE DOE 6

Age when allegedly raped by Nygard: Fifteen

In August 2008, Jane Doe 6 was invited to Nygard Cay by the Nygard Cay DJ, a man that went by the stage name "Shorts."

Despite being underage, Jane Doe 6 "had multiple alcoholic beverages" at the party, according to the lawsuit. Since she "saw several other children that she knew at the party," the lawsuit suggests, she felt somewhat at ease.

Then, she was introduced to Nygard. "Within minutes of the introduction," the lawsuit claims, "Nygard spun her around and said, 'Nice ass.'"

Later, the suit claims, "Nygard invited Jane Doe No. 6 to accompany him to get some marijuana to smoke." She remembers that she "was not afraid, because Nygard had a high profile in the Bahamas, and she held him in high regard."

They went up to his bedroom, she says, and he got into the jacuzzi.

Jane Doe 6 declined to get in as she "began to feel lightheaded from the alcoholic drinks that she had consumed," the lawsuit continues.

Nygard allegedly brushed aside her concern and told her to "get comfortable."

The lawsuit continues:

> Nygard opened a drawer filled with pills and told Jane Doe No. 6 to take some, but she declined. Nygard then untied her bathing suit and began undressing her.
>
> He told her that he wanted her to defecate on his face, and she told him no. Nygard began fondling Jane Doe No. 6 and pushed his finger into her anus. Jane Doe No. 6 tried to fight Nygard off, but he became more aggressive the more that she fought.
>
> He then attempted to have anal sex with Jane Doe No. 6 but was unable to penetrate her anus. He then penetrated her vagina and proceeded to rape her. Jane Doe No. 6 told Nygard

to stop many times and continued to fight, but he overpowered her.

After Nygard was done, Jane Doe No. 6 got dressed immediately and tried to leave the room. Before she could leave, Nygard told her to take a handful of cash. . . . Jane Doe No. 6 refused the cash and left the room. She found her friends and left Nygard Cay.

She never returned.

JANE DOE 7

Age when allegedly raped by Nygard: Eighteen

Jane Doe 7, like others in this lawsuit, was invited to a pamper party by a friend. Once on the property, she took advantage of the open bar.

While Jane Doe 7 was sipping a drink by the beach, the lawsuit claims, "Nygard approached her and introduced himself to her. He then led her upstairs to his bedroom."

They both got into the jacuzzi, the lawsuit says, where "Nygard made sexual advances toward her . . . she resisted."

Then, he allegedly gave her a drink that he had made himself.

"Within several minutes, Jane Doe No. 7 began feeling nauseous and sleepy," the lawsuit claims. Instead of offering her any help, Nygard allegedly "asked her to urinate in his mouth."

Jane Doe 7 says she collapsed on the bed "because she could no longer stand." She claims she "does not recall what happened next because she kept slipping in and out of consciousness," but it wasn't just a catnap.

"She awoke with pain in her anus and blood in her underwear," the lawsuit states. Nygard gave her $550 and allegedly "sent her away." She left Nygard Cay and never returned.

JANE DOE 8

Age when allegedly raped by Nygard: Twenty-nine

Jane Doe 8 was a valued employee at Nygard Cay from 2008 to 2014. Among her duties were "driving to pick up girls who didn't have a ride to a pamper party, hosting pamper parties, recruiting women for pamper parties, and performing household duties at Nygard Cay," she recalls.

The lawsuit claims that Jane Doe 8 "was aware of Nygard's sexual appetites, since she often was the one picking up victims and driving them to and from Nygard Cay. She herself had turned down Nygard's sexual advances many times during the course of her employment at Nygard Cay."

But for years, she had thought that she was safe. In 2014, all that would change.

One day, out of the blue, one of Nygard's "girlfriends" offered Jane Doe 8 a glass of wine.

"The girlfriend was insistent, and although Jane Doe No. 8 rarely drinks at work, she accepted a glass of wine and gulped it down quickly," the suit states.

Not long after, the lawsuit alleges, "she noticed her arms become numb and then she fell unconscious on Nygard's bed. When she became alert again, Nygard was on top of her on his bed and was in the act of penetrating her vaginally with his penis. She was powerless to stop him."

"While slipping in and out of consciousness, Jane Doe No. 8 saw three specific girlfriends walk in and witness what was happening, including the girlfriend who provided her the wine. When Jane Doe No. 8 finally became fully awake, she left the household, went out to her car, and began crying."

Jane Doe 8 was trapped, forced to continue working at Nygard Cay "out of financial necessity," according to the lawsuit. She did her best to avoid him, and she says that before long Nygard noticed.

"Nygard finally confronted her about the rape and told her 'not to take it personally.' Eventually, Nygard told Jane Doe No. 8 that she must either continue to have sex with him regularly, or that she would no longer be employed. When she refused," the lawsuit claims, "she was terminated."

But her nightmare was not over.

On April 6, 2017, Jane Doe 8 was taking out the trash at her house "when she was accosted by two of Nygard's employees," the lawsuit claims. "The two employees stated that Nygard wanted to speak to her and that she needed to travel to see him."

Jane Doe 8 made it clear that she wasn't interested in a reunion. Still, the suit continues, "The employees ignored her refusal and used physical force to take her inside, confiscate her passport, and put her into a car. She had no clothes or travel items with her."

Confused and scared, she "was driven by the two employees to the airport and given a plane ticket to fly to Toronto. When she arrived," the lawsuit claims, "she was only wearing shorts and a T-shirt and was freezing. She was forced into a hotel room and restrained or guarded to prevent escape."

"During this time, her cell phone was confiscated, and she was not allowed to let her family or friends know where she was. Nygard, however, did not appear in Toronto and the employees who abducted her provided plane tickets, and at Nygard's instruction, took her to Fort Lauderdale."

There, the lawsuit claims, she was "restrained and guarded in another hotel room under the guise of speaking to Nygard." Nygard still never showed, and they flew her back to Nassau on April 10. From that day forward, Jane Doe 8 would live in fear for her life.

(While the story of Jane Doe 8 is nearly identical to that of Richette Ross, she is not identified in the complaint.)

JANE DOE 9

Age when allegedly raped by Nygard: "Adult"

Jane Doe 9 is a US citizen who worked for Nygard and the Nygard Companies in the U.S.. "Over the years," the lawsuit claims, "she was sexually assaulted by Nygard on numerous occasions."

"On each occasion, she would resist and tell him no, but he would force himself on her," the suit alleges.

In just one example of such an alleged assault, Jane Doe 9 allegedly "was raped by Nygard at his residence in Marina del Rey, California," in 2015.

Her allegations echoed the claims of former Nygard employees from long before: "She was asleep in a guest room that had a key code lock on the door," the suit claims. "Nygard overrode the key code and entered the room without her permission while she was sleeping."

"She awoke to Nygard forcefully and physically overpowering her as she attempted to stop him from raping her. She verbally demanded he stop, but he refused and proceeded to forcefully penetrate her."

After that night, Jane Doe 9 says she "sought medical treatment" and "eventually left her employment with Nygard and the Nygard Companeis due to the continuous sexual assault that she endured."

"She did not report Nygard's sexual abuse," the suit explains, "because she is extremely scared of him and what he might do to her."

JANE DOE 10

Age when allegedly raped by Nygard: Fifteen

Jane Doe 10 had heard girls talking about the "pamper parties," the lawsuit explains, "and thought that they sounded fun." When she was fifteen years old, her sister invited her to come to a "pamper party" at Nygard Cay, and she jumped at the opportunity. Like so many others, she had no idea what awaited her.

"After eating sushi and grilled meats, Jane Doe No. 10 noticed that she was not feeling well and was nauseous," the lawsuit claims. "She was approached by Nygard and his security guard shortly thereafter. Nygard held Jane Doe No. 10's hand and told her to follow him. Jane Doe No. 10 asked why, but Nygard refused to answer and dragged her along with them."

The lawsuit continues:

Nygard's security guard walked with them as they arrived at what Jane Doe No. 10 soon realized was Nygard's bedroom. She became afraid. After she and Nygard entered the bedroom, Nygard's security guard stood outside his door.

Once they were alone in the room, Nygard commented on Jane Doe No. 10's body, told her that she could be a model for him, and cupped her butt with his hands. Nygard then told her to take off her clothes.

Jane Doe No. 10 told Nygard that she was not comfortable doing that, as she was only 15 years old.

Feeling "dizzy and light-headed," she told Nygard that she was not feeling well, and that she was ready to go home. Nygard opened a drawer and took out a small white pill. He told Jane Doe No. 10 to take the pill, lie down, and it would make her feel better. She did.

Nygard then asked Jane Doe No. 10 if she had ever had anal sex before. She told him that she had never heard of that before. Nygard told Jane Doe No. 10 that she was going to like it, and offered her $5,000.

Nygard then forced Jane Doe No. 10 onto the bed and climbed on top of her, kissing her neck and breast. Jane Doe No. 10 told him that he was making her feel uncomfortable.

Jane Doe No. 10 tried to fight Nygard off of her, but he physically overpowered her. The harder she fought, the angrier he got. Jane Doe No. 10 became overwhelmed.

Nygard then forced his penis into her vagina. It was very painful and Jane Doe No. 10 began to cry. Jane Doe No. 10 told Nygard that he was hurting her and that she was still not feeling well. Nygard told Jane Doe No. 10 to lie down on her stomach and she would feel better. Jane Doe No. 10 laid down on her stomach and Nygard immediately laid on her back and started kissing her neck.

Nygard then offered Jane Doe No. 10 $10,000 to defecate into his mouth. Jane Doe No. 10 responded that she could not do that and that she was in a lot of pain. Nygard then forced his penis into Jane Doe No. 10's anus.

When he was done, Jane Doe No. 10 immediately left the room and went downstairs to her sister. Jane Doe No. 10's sister could tell that she was visibly upset, but she did not tell her what had happened. They went home and Jane Do No. 10 did not tell anyone what had happened because she was scared and embarrassed.

Jane Doe No. 10 woke up the following day and she was bleeding from her anus. She was too afraid to tell her mother, so she asked her sister to accompany her to the doctor. Jane Doe No. 10 had to receive two stitches in her anus to stop the bleeding.

She didn't report the incident to the authorities.

Nygard's attorney, Jay Prober, has announced that he will move to have the lawsuit struck down, claiming it "has no foundation, that it's scandalacious, that it's vexatious and it doesn't deserve the time of day in court." By press time, more than a month after the complaint was first filed, he hasn't filed any response yet.

***

The lawsuit landed at first with a rippple. Media court reporters, not necessarily aware of the name Peter Nygard, may have overlooked it for the time being. All that changed on February 22, 2020, when more than a million people saw the front page of the most widely-read paper in the English-speaking world, the *New York Times*. In the top lefthand corner of the Sunday paper—the most exclusive real estate in print—was a stunning exposé by three *Times* reporters about the *true* Peter Nygard. Going far beyond just the lawsuit, the reporters had interviewed more than 270 people in Nygard's orbit over the past twelve months. They spent time in Canada, the Bahamas, and New York on the hunt. The results spoke for themselves.

Only the first in a series, this article was explosive. The series not only put the Jane Doe federal lawsuit front and center in the public consciousness but also documented—fact by fact and testimony by testimony—the tip of the iceberg of Nygard's history of sexual predation. The many allegations of assault were truly vile. The stories of his perverse pyramid schemes— whereby young victims were induced to recruit new victims—were utterly nauseating. With this series of articles, a bright, shining spotlight finally swung to illuminate an evil corner that had been dark for far too long. The world was introduced to Peter Nygard, sexual psychopath, by the most respected journalistic source in the business.

The *Times* reporters weren't the only ones investigating, though. The February 22 article mentioned that the FBI had looked into Nygard twice. Even more shockingly, the *Times* disclosed that there had been a nine-month investigation by the Department of Homeland Security (DHS) into Nygard's sex-trafficking activities. The US prosecutorial system has had an almost totally dysfunctional history when it has come to actually prosecuting cases of sexual abuse—especially if the perpetrator is a white, well-connected predator. To that end, it was perhaps not entirely suprising that the *Times* revealed that those investigations had mysteriously "fizzled." (The writers went no further to explain. The backstory of what happened with the DHS investigators—and how the Nevada US Attorney's Office was involved— deserves its own separate book. Stay tuned!)

Also striking was a blurb in the February 22 article concerning one victim in particular, Marvinique Smith. Marvinique and her sister, Maronique, had broken down emotionally when detailing allegations of how they both had been abused by Nygard. When Marvinique confessed that she had been sodomized by Nygard at the age of ten years old after being lured to Nygard's bedroom at Nygard Cay by way of an offer to watch cartoons, even the reporters were in tears. In addition to describing their traumatic abuse to the *Times*, the sisters had reported the sexual abuse allegations to the Bahamian police, and had also told their stories to several sets of investigators and lawyers.

Reportedly, the *New York Times* was originally set to run their article in November 2019—this, despite two threatening letters from Nygard's lawyers stating that the *New York Times* would be the object of a $500 million defamation lawsuit if they ran with their story. This wasn't enough to deter them from revealing the truth. A harsher blow was delivered, as a March 6 story described, when "a reporter's worst nightmare" came true. When the reporters went back to the Bahamas one last time in early November to double- and triple-check their facts, they set up a meeting with the Smith sisters. By this time, the reporters felt that they had bonded with the girls and could trust them completely. When the girls showed up for the interview, the reporters were stunned by the journalistic equivalent of a knife in the gut: "We're sorry, but we were lying about everything we told you," the sisters said. "We have never been to Nygard Cay. We were never abused. We have never even met Mr. Nygard. Sorry."

Even though the Smith sisters were now self-confessed liars, this bombshell stopped the *Times* article in its tracks. The reporters were likely doubting every other interview they'd done. Were there other victims out there, women whom these reporters had relied on, who could end up recanting such stories after publication? As bad as it was to hear such a confession *before* publication, hearing it *after* the story was already all over the newsstands and the internet would be a debacle.

It took a few weeks, but the reporters began to compile damning circumstantial evidence that rebutted the Smith sisters' recanted testimony, and their claims that Richette Ross had paid them to lie.

First, as the March 6, 2020, *Times* article described, Ross voluntarily took and passed a lie detector test in which she testified that she had not paid anyone to lie.

Second, two ex-Nygard exmployees whom the *Times* had reason to trust both testified that they had seen the Smith sisters at a Nygard Cay party. One of these ex-employees had been the same ComCor executive who had arranged for the girls to be invited to, and accepted into, the pamper parties at Nygard Cay.

Most intriguing of all, however, was a conversation that the *Times* uncovered between an unnamed source and Nygard's most trusted insider within the Royal Bahamas Police Force: an officer named Camalo McCoy. McCoy had somehow obtained an audio copy of a sensitive internal interview which lawyer and victims' advocate Fred Smith had conducted with Marvinique Smith in his law office during which she dramatically and emotionally detailed Nygard's abuse of both her and her sister. McCoy provided a copy of this audiotape to Nygard, so both Nygard and McCoy were aware of the girl's testimony. Given the rumors of Nygard's ruthless side, this was not a good development for the Smith sisters.

The *Times* obtained yet another audio conversation between McCoy and an unnamed source, in which he said:

> I let Nygard listen to [the Fred Smith and Martinique Smith conversation] and he said "Man I don't . . . I don't even remember that name."
>
> And then I get my guy to go and look for this person. He find the person. And we questioned the person.
>
> We was trying to get the person to admit that Richette Ross set them up to say this thing. You see? So they could make that up. They fabricate some things.

The ploy ultimately backfired. The overwhelming circumstantial evidence documented that Nygard had once again turned to a corrupt police official in the Bahamas and that one or more police officers had either successfully bribed or successfully threatened a key victim in both the *New York Times* story and the police department's own investigation of Peter Nygard.

The reporters even faced such intimidation themselves, they wrote in the March 6 piece. The process of reporting their series had been one filled with thinly veiled threats, faked names, and strange happenings.

In the process of reporting this book, our investigators faced similar roadblocks. In one case, we were told to meet with a source who had knowledge of the pamper parties, only to arrive and be confronted with a Nygard loyalist ranting, raving, and acting very physically aggressive. Other sources warned us to keep a low profile and be careful who we spoke to.

If reporters from thousands of miles away could face such pressure in the fight to reveal the truth, imagine the level of fear and even danger that all of the alleged victims faced in coming forward. Their courage knows no bounds, and if—under threat—they were to recant their statements and desperately try to return to normal life, one could hardly blame them.

In the meantime, still more women have come forward to add their stories to the ones told in the lawsuit.

TAMIRA

Age when allegedly raped by Nygard: Fifteen

Life growing up in the Bahamas was "fun" for Tamira, who told her story in an interview recorded for this book. She played basketball, enjoyed school, and dreamed of being "a music artist."

"Everyone looked out for each other," she said, and her world felt small and safe.

By the time she was a teen, Tamira said, "I had heard about the parties" at Nygard Cay. When one of her friends invited her, she jumped on the opportunity.

The party was fun at first, but quickly shifted. Nygard approached and led her and her friend to a jacuzzi. Tamira explained, "We were wearing bathing suits. I was facing him in the jacuzzi."

Nygard turned predatory almost as soon as she sat down, she claims, asking her to "stroke him." His next request was even more disturbing, she alleges: "He just came out and said it, 'Shit on me.'"

"I just couldn't believe it," Latira said. Her friend "tried" to complete the act, she claims, but she couldn't. Instead, Tamira alleges, Nygard raped her.

"It wasn't really that long" before he was done with her, she said. Nygard allegedly handed over cash and she headed to the bathroom, in pain. She left, and carried the secret with her for years.

"I didn't want to talk about it," she explained, fear and shame still choking her voice. "I would be judged."

She didn't even tell the police, Tamira said, because she had little hope for justice. She explained, "I would think they wouldn't take seriously what I said."

That one night had altered the course of Tamira's life forever. "It changed how I handle relationships and stuff," she said.

Only recently has she found some solace in sharing her story. Speaking out alongside her fellow victims, she said, "I felt no more alone."

TAMIKA

Age when allegedly raped by Nygard: Sixteen

Tamika Ferguson came forward to tell her story to the *New York Times* just as the Jane Doe lawsuit was being filed. The newspaper praised her for having the courage to put her name to her allegations—one of the first women to do so.

Tamika was an orphan and a high school dropout when a local DJ invited her to a Nygard Cay pamper party in 2004.

According to the *Times*, "She drank too much and ended up in a bathroom barefoot in her bikini, she said. When she emerged, her friends had gone. She said Mr. Nygard steered her upstairs and raped her."

That was only the beginning of Ferguson's torture, she said. According to her claims, Nygard continued to send drivers to her home to pick her up for parties. She continued to go, and says she continued to have sex with him. Although she "chose" to go, most people by now understand that a sexual encounter between a man pushing 75 and a teenager could hardly ever be considered consensual. The fact that Ferguson had no parents and, as a dropout, no future laid out ahead of her made her particularly vulnerable to such exploitation.

"He messed with my whole life," Ferguson told *The Times*. "And everybody knew what was going on except for me."

THE TEACHER

Age when allegedly raped by Nygard: Fifteen

According to a source who knows her, the kindergarten teacher is the picture of a composed professional. Confident and composed, she has been able to hide any trace of the dark secrets that haunt her, the story of what she claims happened to her at Nygard Cay.

The source said that the teacher was only fifteen when she went to a pamper party with a group of friends. In her neighborhood, Nygard was seen as a little bit of a superhero. All she knew of him was what she saw on TV: He was rich, glamorous, and constantly doling out cash.

She described her first impressions of his Nygard Cay property to Ryan Thorpe of the *Winnipeg Free Press*. "I had never, never saw anything like that in my life," she told Thorpe. "Paradise wasn't paradise . . . it was hell."

"Two cups" of Baileys Irish Cream liqueur was enough to lower her defenses. Before long, she found herself in Nygard's bedroom. "Stuck on You" by Lionel Richie—a past guest of Nygard Cay—was playing on repeat. That would be the soundtrack, the teacher says, to her rape.

"I just laid there with tears rolling down my face," she told Thorpe. "And I just cried until he stopped."

The schoolteacher never told a soul about what happened. A source confirmed, however, that she recorded details of the alleged incident in a diary she kept at the time. Far from just one offhand entry—the kind that could easily be faked—the schoolteacher's entries from this period are only part of a much bigger collection of handwritten memories that she kept during her teen years.

Breaking down in tears, she told Thorpe, "I told God that I did not know that we had these kinds of monsters in this world."

As horrifying the stories of these girls and women are, they are just the beginning. The lawsuit claims that Nygard's pamper parties were only the foundation for an even wider, more sophisticated sex-trafficking ring. For the women ensnared in its web, the nightmare didn't end with one night at Nygard Cay.

CHAPTER 10
THE MILE-HIGH CLUB

The only time you are working is when you wish you were doing something else.
—Peter Nygard

Former Nygard employees have claimed that their boss rarely targeted the same girl twice at Nygard Cay. Some, though, allegedly were forced to relive their personal nightmare day in and day out as long-term members of what Nygard called his "harem."

According to the Jane Doe lawsuit, "the victims that Nygard found most attractive and sexually desirable were forced through a combination of fraud, coercion, psychological force and manipulation, and physical force . . . to become full-time sex workers, which he referred to as his 'girlfriends.'"

At any given time, the group of women by Nygard's side could include girls he'd recruited in the Bahamas, models flown in from the US and Canada, and Eastern European beauties. Usually, there were at least three in his traveling group. Looking at photographs of his red carpet appearances posted on the Nygard website, the faces change over the years even as some elements of the scene stayed the same.

In every photo, the women are dazzling—if somewhat dead in the eyes. Clad in gowns and designer gear, they gaze into the cameras surrounding them. They traveled with Nygard to California, New Orleans, New York, Tucson, London, Berlin, or Toronto.

From the outside, it seemed impossibly glamorous. On the inside, the lawsuit claims, it was hell.

According to the suit, Nygard's "girlfriends" were initially "led to believe that they are traveling with him as models on glamourous fashion tours. Eventually, they learn that they are nothing more thatn full-time sex workers for Nygard that are forced to cater to all of his personal needs, including his demands for sex acts."

It was a twenty-four-hour-a-day job, and the alleged job description was ever-changing. The lawsuit claims:

> They must awake every day at 5:30 a.m. to prepare his breakfast and ensure that it is ready for him to eat the moment he awakens. They are also required to, among other things, give him his medications on schedule, prepare his clothes, bathe him, clip his toenails, and prepare all of his meals . . . to prepare his bags with marketing and public relations materials for his business meetings relating to the Nygard Companies, attend his business meetings, otherwise act as his personal servants, and to model company clothing for company executives.
>
> [They] are expected to constantly go out and buy the tools of Nygard's trade: condoms, lubricants, and the Plan B abortion pill.

That was all in addition to the requirement that they satisfy the main requirement, what the lawsuit called Nygard's "perverse sexual desires."

Nygard often brought his "girlfriends" to New York City, for example, where his flagship store lorded over Times Square and he kept an apartment on an upper floor. When in the city, the complaint alleges, the women were subjected to an entirely different level of abuse as Nygard brought them to Manhattan's underground swingers clubs.

Nygard "regularly forced his 'girlfriends' to accompany him to 'swingers' clubs in New York City," the suit alleges.

"While at the 'swingers' clubs, Nygard forced his 'girlfriends' to find couples for him to have sex with. He then paid, forced, and or coerced his 'girlfriends' to have sex with other men, while he watched and engaged in sex with the mens' partners."

As if that weren't enough, the most perverse duty for Nygard's "harem" was one that ironically, did not require them to get naked. After subjecting themselves to rape, sodomy, and worse, the lawsuit claims, Nygard would then flip these women and ask them to "recruit" or "procure" other girls and women that Nygard could abuse as well.

"Nygard refers to his newly recruited victims as 'fresh meat' or 'sacrifices," the lawsuit alleges, and not just any girl would do.

According to the suit, "Nygard has an expressed desire for children and tells his 'girlfriends' who 'recruit' for him, 'the younger the better.'"

The girls' duty didn't end with delivering these children to their horrible fate. The lawsuit claims, "Nygard fully expects his 'girlfriends' to 'loosen up' his victims by giving them alcohol laced with drugs, including mind-altering drugs."

For this, the women say, they were compensated handsomely. "Harem" members "were paid monthly through direct deposit with funds from a Nygard corporate account by the Nygard corporate accountant," the suit alleges. The women have said they submitted invoices for "modeling and promotional services," even though the true extent of their work happened far beyond any red carpet.

As for their salary, "the amounts of their payments were based upon their level of servitude to Nygard, their ability to satisfy his sexual desires, and their ability to 'recruit' new victims for him to engage in commercial sex acts with," the lawsuit claims.

These women were not just looking for a paycheck, though. Mostly, they say they did what they had to do in those years out of pure terror. According to the lawsuit, Nygard kept "tight and coercive control over his 'girlfriends' through a variety of direct and indirect manipulation tactics, including threats of force, physical intimidation and abuse, verbal abuse, forced labor, withholding payment, and confiscating travel documents."

For example, since the women's travel arrangements were made by the Nygard Companies, they have claimed they often found themselves abroad in foreign countries with no money and no passport. They had no idea of how they would get home if they managed to escape—or worse, were abandoned. Those who refused his orders, the lawsuit says, were often left behind "broke and destitute," a warning for those who remained by his side.

What awaited those who remained? If they failed "to provide Nygard with an easily exploitable victim each night," the lawsuit alleges, Nygard punished them "by verbally berating them, inflicting psychological abuse, withholding or cutting pay, forcing them to do manual labor, and forcing them to satisfy his perverse sexual desires."

On the other hand, the ones that delivered were "paid extra" and were "able to avoid his wrath and sometimes avoid being his sexual victim," the lawsuit claimed. It was a terrible calculus that forced these women to choose between the shame and pain of their own continued victimization and the guilt of sacrificing others to the same fate. So many chose the latter, saddling themselves with yet another layer of trauma that would take years to begin to heal.

Truly understanding these women's mind-set, though, requires an understanding of the culture from whence they came. While some were from the US or Canada, most were handpicked from the tropics—a place where they were practically raised to keep rape and sexual assault to themselves.

According to the 2020 US State Department Human Rights Report, violence against women in the Bahamas "continues to be a serious, widespread problem." As recently as 2007, the small island nation had the highest rate of rapes in the world, and in 2018, the US State Department issued a travel advisory warning for tourists that "sexual assault is common" in the Bahamas.

Complicating the issue is the fact that as much as 95 percent of rapes go unreported worldwide. In the Bahamas, the Jane Doe lawsuit explained, rape "is particularly underreported . . . due to a culture of stigmatization, victim shaming, government corruption, and weakly-enforced laws."

For example, in 2013, the Bahamas Crisis Centre reported having counseled 122 new clients for rape and 42 for sexual assault; the Emergency Room at Princess Margaret Hospital reported treating nearly 150 rape cases at their facility. During that same period, the police recorded only 104 rapes for the entire country.

Why the disparity? According to the Jane Doe lawsuit, "The word for rape in the Bahamas is 'hush.' It is not discussed or spoken of as a societal problem."

In the island's highly patriarchal culture, sexual violence against women is often regarded as a private matter. Spousal rape was not even considered a crime until 2007. Even today, it is not considered a crime unless the assault occurs while the parties are legally separated.

Those that do muster the courage to report the crimes perpetrated against them only rarely find justice. According to a report compiled by the Inter-American Development Bank, "On average, the percentage of rape cases solved between 2010 and 2013 was 40 percent, while homicides for the same period had a clearance rate of 61 percent. This means rapes are highly unlikely to be prosecuted, which does little to stimulate better reporting."

In short, why put yourself through the pain of publicly revealing your most painful secrets, if it won't make a difference anyway?

For women in particular, the hopelessness of their situation as victims is often compounded by the wider corruption that affects all Bahamian citizens.

Indeed, it wasn't just Nygard who was indulging in political payoffs, favors, and power grabs.

In April 2016, the *Bahamas Tribune* reported on a survey by Transparency International that found that corruption is "rooted in the fabric of Bahamian society."

According to that survey of 1,000 Bahamians, one in ten citizens had been forced to pay a bribe within the past year to obtain public services. Only about 6 percent of the people surveyed admitted to actually reporting corruption when they experienced it. And of those, not one person who reported corruption ever saw the authorities take action against the government officials involved.

When asked why Bahamians traditionally do not report corruption, 44 percent of survey respondents said they were "too afraid of the consequences." Another 19 percent said they felt that "nothing will be done" anyways, and 7 percent were concerned that the officials they would have to report to "are also corrupt." Roughly 5 percent explained that they didn't report because corruption is "normal" in the Bahamas, and "everyone does it."

In response to the survey, Lemarque Campbell, Chair of Citizens for a Better Bahamas, told the paper that corruption had become "a cultural element in the mindset of Bahamians."

In all, it was the perfect environment to keep crimes against women hidden in the sand. The Jane Does' attorney explained, "Victims of sexual crimes in the Bahamas rarely pursue their claims. They are ashamed and embarrassed, fear retaliation and victimization, rightfully do not trust law enforcement to pursue and prosecute their attackers, and do not trust the court system to provide them with justice."

It was a situation that some say that Nygard exploited.

"Nygard made a concentrated and deliberate effort to protect and conceal his criminal activities," the Jane Doe complaint alleged. Beyond his political payoffs, Nygard's alleged victims recalled that "in an effort to reinforce fear, control and dominance . . . Nygard regularly flaunted his political power to control the Bahamian police and the Bahamian government by inviting and parading government officials at his Nygard Cay property and in front of Nygard's victims."

Community leader Reverend C. B. Moss said in an interview recorded for this book that it was a scheme that worked. "Everything was quite on the down low," he said. "It's only now that people are even beginning to voice it publicly."

"Everything was so quiet, so secret," Moss continued. "In fact, it was such a sort of secret operation."

"You must appreciate that that operation being held in Lyford Cay was away from the average community. And it was not only physically removed, but it's psychologically it was another world," he explained. "So people did not focus on that. And even if they heard something," they wouldn't take the rumor seriously.

In addition to Nygard's darker pursuits, Moss said, Nygard helped to build the impenetrable wall around his dark world by showering the community with charitable donations and hosting events. "Mr. Nygard was viewed as a generous individual who supported community projects and such," Moss said. "He had achieved a bit of good will amongst the people."

In addition to the pamper parties, Nygard hosted local kids' summer camps and church groups at Nygard Cay for field days, this investigation found. One group was a camp run by retired boxer Jimmy "Killer" Coakley. (Coakley was later remanded to prison over human trafficking and rape charges himself.)

One of Nygard's most effective local PR moves over the years was to sponsor the 2000 Olympic women's 4x400 relay team, known in the press as "The Golden Girls." Nygard donated $25,000 to their cause, and offered to match any amount raised by other local corporations.

At the team's big send-off event, twenty-year veteran team member Pauline Davis Thompson gave a monologue praising their "benefactor."

"To me," she said, "you are a Bahamian. And I want to say to you that when we go to Australia, we are going to do our very best. We are going to run our hearts out. We are going to make the United States run the race of its life. We come from a small nation, but we come from a powerful nation."

Another team member, Chandra Sturrup, "assured Nygard the financial contribution he made . . . would go a long way." Nygard didn't just offer a financial contribution. According to team member Debbie Ferguson-McKenzie, Nygard "invited the team to a special dinner before the race," to give "them an 'attitude check.'"

Whatever he did, it worked. The team won Gold in Sydney, and the Golden Girls continued to collect medals over the next several years. They collected checks from Nygard, too. In 2009, he gave Ferguson-McKenzie checks totaling $7,500 as a reward when she was part of the silver-medal-winning team at the IAAF World Championships.

At the check presentation ceremony, a reporter for the *Bahamas Press* wrote, "All of the athletes present stated that Nygard has never asked for anything in return except that they perform at their best and make the Bahamas proud."

For these reasons and more, Nygard all but owned almost everyone on the island, from the Prime Minister down to the girls playing sports in the streets.

Even customs officials were said to be under his thumb. According to the Jane Doe lawsuit, Nygard "regularly bribes Bahamian officials . . . to prevent customs from searching his plane, prevent customs from checking the passports of young women onboard, and to prevent customs from inspecting the passengers' luggage."

"This allows Nygard to traffic his victims to and from the Bahamas, transport drugs intended for his victims, and transport other supplies for 'pamper parties' in the Nygard Companies' planes to avoid paying customs."

Nygard's jet wasn't just a plane in the same way that Nygard Cay wasn't just a beach house. Built in 1970 and fully upgraded over the years, the "N-Force" jet was a massive Boeing 727. True to form, Nygard had his name painted across the entire side of the plane, and a made-up "N-Force" seal on the tail.

"His paint scheme makes Trump's ego look modest," one plane-watcher said in an online forum.

Inside, the jet made Jeffrey Epstein's "Lolita Express" look like a Spirit Air flight. A source close to Nygard provided interior photos of the jet for this book, and they are truly jaw-dropping.

First of all, nearly every hard surface inside the plane is covered with gleaming silver and blue chrome. Even the ceilings were mirrored, so guests lying down on the beds and banquettes spread throughout the plane could take commemorative selfies.

"Nygard N-Force" seals are painted on the walls, alongside massive blown-up photos of Nygard posing with some of the world's most famous people: Anna Nicole Smith, Pamela Anderson, Richard Branson, Serena Williams, Iman, and even former President George H. W. Bush, among them.

Despite all of the unusual features, one could hardly miss the plane's main attraction: a glistening chrome stripper pole. Surrounded by strippers, and with a circle of what appeared to be hard wood at its base, the pole was perfectly situated for a performance. A low table with four cushioned armchairs was positioned just inches from the pole, near enough to touch anyone on it. The backdrop for the scene was a large projection screen behind the pole, which could be used for screening movies. Nygard was allegedly known to be a big fan of porn.

The jet could seat thirteen regular passengers and eight VIPs, according to flight records obtained for this book. Who was lucky (or unlucky) enough to catch a ride?

According to flight manifests obtained from a source, Nygard took more than twenty flights in one typical three-month period, and scarcely a flight took off without a pretty young female on board. In one period, the manifest lists the following roster of females, most born in the 1980s:

- 82 Americans
- 22 Canadians
- 4 Bahamians
- 2 Brazilians
- 2 Czechs
- 1 Belgian
- 1 Estonian
- 1 Dominican
- 1 Ethiopian
- 1 Lebanese
- 1 Ukrainian
- 1 Yemeni

None appeared to be underage, but three of the female passengers were listed with no age: Claudia, Latifah, and Monica.

The flight manifests reveal that Nygard most frequently traveled to LA, Toronto, Amsterdam, Cologne, London, Nassau, Hong Kong and Beijing. He also made frequent stops in Curitiba and Florianopolis, Brazil. Among the stranger destinations were Dhaka, Bangladesh—where Nygard claimed to have a sales office and production plant. He also stopped in Petropavlosk, Russia. The reason for his stop there is unclear.

Nygard's male business colleagues also often hopped a ride with him and his "harem." Unlike Jeffrey Epstein, however, he wasn't exactly transporting world leaders. Nygard's passengers were decidedly more down market. In addition to several male Nygard employees, flight manifests show flights taken by the following passengers, for example: Sugar Hill Gang DJ David Gunthorpe; Bob Bresnahan, designer of the Skye's the Limit fashion line (a Dillard's favorite); and Jon Baram, president of Warren & Baram Management, "which specializes in the representation of Latina and African-American talent."

Perhaps the most frequent traveler during this period, though, was Suelyn Medeiros. An Instagram model, she's been linked to singer Chris Brown, rapper Nelly, and NFL star Deral Boykin over the years. In roughly four months of flight manifests reviewed for this book, she took nearly thirty trips with Nygard, flying to New York, Toronto, and even Oklahoma City. Medeiros made no secret of her relationship with Nygard, grinning in photos with him at red carpet events. Today, she's a mom and models for Fashion Nova, among others.

Medeiros wrote about her time with Nygard in her 2014 memoir. At first, she remembers, Nygard seemed like a knight in shining armor. Medeiros says she was leaving an abusive relationship and planning a move to California when her agent called with an intriguing offer: "A fashion designer owned an island there. He was letting people use it for the shoot, and a magazine was booking it for several days."

"I'd heard about the island and its reputation for wild parties, so I was hesitant," she writes. It was only a two-day trip, though, so she bit the bullet and flew down. Pretty quickly, she realized her intuition had been right.

"The photo shoot wasn't quite as organized or professional as my agent had painted it," Medeiros claims. "It seemed more like a giant party, but it was only two days so what could happen?"

The drinks were flowing and there were "half-naked girls dancing in the sand. I was apprehensive," Medeiros remembers. "It seemed shady to me, a little "Bachhanalish."

She was sitting by the pool, sipping a Coke and planning her imminent departure, when Nygard approached. Medeiros says, "He was trying to be very charming and he was. I was also trying to let him know that I was all about business." In no uncertain terms, Medeiros told Nygard that she was uncomfortable with what was unfolding at Nygard Cay, and she wanted to go home. He was incredibly accommodating, and Medeiros was surprised.

"I will admit that he was charming," she writes. "He sounded kind, not aggressive, and seemed genuinely interested in me. He told me to stay in touch and call him when I got to California, that he might be able to help me a little."

The only problem with Medeiros's big LA plan was that she didn't even have an apartment yet, and she admitted that much to the billionaire designer. Before she knew it, she was agreeing to move into his Marina Del Rey mansion.

"I had to admit, he was convincing," Madeiros says. "I really had nothing to lose and he could be an incredible boost to my career with his own line and all his connections. The kicker was when he offered to fly me (and all of my things) out on his private plane."

Once in California, it all seemed too good to be true. The house was "stunning," and Nygard pretty much left her alone. Sometimes he'd check in for phone chats, but Medeiros says she was "grateful" for his advice. In the meantime, "Peter's perks" included a red Ferrari, a Hummer, DeLorean, BMW, and American Express card with an eye-wateringly high limit. Still, the two were still on a friendship level—at least in Medeiros's mind.

She got a jolt of reality on New Year's Eve 2006. Nygard had given Medeiros and her friends an all-expenses-paid trip to Brazil. At the stroke of midnight, he came to collect. "Peter turned to me and gave me a light kiss on the lips," Madeiros claims. "I immediately froze but so that I wouldn't embarrass him, I smiled, tittered like a litte girl, and went off to join my friends who were dancing."

After that moment, Medeiros's relationship with Nygard changed. It began to feel awkward, she writes, and even potentially dangerous. She wrote in her diary, "These wide open spaces are not mine, but are instead a constant reminder that I owe him, all the time. "

She continued, "I fear and know that nothing is free, but you can get a lot of it if you're not careful what you ask for; and then, when you least expect it if you're not prepared it'll be time to pay the piper. *What will he ask of me? What will I have to do?*"

"All I want to do is leave Peter's and not depend on him. The longer I live here in this mansion, the more I owe him. Yes, everything is free and I don't have to do anything, but I fear the day will come soon when that will change."

Once carefree and scarcely able to believe her luck, Medeiros began to find living under Nygard's thumb totally intolerable—like a frog, she says, being boiled alive. On the one hand, she was so grateful for the gifts and business lessons he had given her. Calling him "my official cheerleader," she admits, "he tutored me well."

But "behind that smile and those twinkling eyes was a very calculating, smart, and aggressive man," Medeiros wrote, "who peed on every bush that surrounded his kingdom, sometimes three times a day." The more she got to know him, the more she began to fear him.

In addition, she admitted, "I began to resent the arm candy thing."

"I was falling into the obligation thing, the guilt thing. He'd helped me so much . . . and yet at times I was nothing more than an attractive piece of flesh, no more no less," she wrote. "I was getting to the point where I didn't want to be seen with him."

Around that time, Medeiros met the man who would become "the love of her life," "Joe." Secretly, she plotted with him to make her escape from Marina Del Rey and Nygard's influence. One day when he was out of town, she packed up all her things and fled. She had escaped unharmed—at least, physically.

***

In Nygard's orbit, the lawsuit alleges, everything he owned and nearly everyone he employed was secretly enabling an international sex trafficking, drug smuggling, and kidnapping ring that had run rampant for decades. For years, it had been unchecked due to the wealth of its perpetrator and the unique cultural vulnerabilities of the country he had chosen for his hunt. Peter Nygard probably thought for a long time that he had gotten away with it all, especially as he watched contemporaries like Jeffrey Epstein go down. But his time was coming.

CHAPTER 11
BUSINESS AS USUAL

There's a thrill in victory. I enjoy the power and position we
operate from today. I never have to walk anywhere with my
cap in hand again.
—Peter Nygard

When the Jane Does filed their lawsuit in New York, it was certainly one of the more explosive filings to hit the city since the days of the Jeffrey Epstein investigation in 2019. But for most Americans—many of whom were unfamiliar with the Canadian designer—it didn't quite break into the news cycle.

All that changed on February 25, as FBI agents, NYPD officers, and members of the US Attorney's Office for the Southern District of New York swarmed Nygard's Times Square headquarters, search warrant in hand. The raid did not come in conjunction with criminal charges, but as officers across the country descended on his Marina del Rey property as well, it seemed that Nygard had certainly caught the feds' interest— perhaps in no small part thanks to the explosive feature in *The New York Times* published only days before.

According to reports, Nygard had been under investigation for nearly six months, as part of a joint child-exploitation task force run out of a US Attorney's Office in New York. When approached for this book, the FBI said they "could not confirm or deny" any ongoing investigation on their part.

Nygard actually confirmed the existence of an ongoing investigation himself, however, when his spokesman released the following statement:

"Nygard welcomes the federal investigation and expects his name to be cleared. He has not been charged, is not in custody, and is participating with the investigation."

For the attorneys representing the Jane Does, it was a victory and vindication. "Given Mr. Nygard's pattern of alleged horrific sexual abuse spanning decades and across the world, it is not surprising that he now finds himself under the scrutiny of the FBI," attorneys Greg Gutzler and Lisa Haba said in a joint statement. "Our focus remains squarely on pursuing justice for the countless victims who have been so viciously harmed by Mr. Nygard and his enablers."

It soon became apparent that there could be more victims than even they knew. In the weeks surrounding the raid, attorneys Gutzler and Haba would hear from more than one hundred new witnesses and dozens of additional victims who claimed to have been sexually assaulted by Nygard.

Nassau community leader Reverend C. B. Moss says he has witnessed that process firsthand on the streets of his community. "You know, similar to the 'Me Too' movement in the United States, once one person starts to talk, it is validation to others and strength for them to come out and talk about it," he said in an interview for this book. "I believe you're going to hear more going forward as more of the participants become bolder and coming out and your chips will fall."

Indeed, it was not just the American attorneys who were bombarded with a wave of new victims following the lawsuit filing and the raid. Back on the island, Royal Bahamas Police Force Commissioner Anthony Ferguson confirmed that his officers had launched an "active investigation" against Nygard. Ferguson declined to clarify the nature of the investigation, only admitting that it was regarding "a reported matter against Peter Nygard."

Nygard's attorney Jay Prober tried to dismiss the news in a statement to the local paper. "Anybody who makes a complaint like that, whether it's true or not, the police are obliged to investigate it," he said. "The investigation will amount to nothing."

However, Nassau attorney Doneth Cartwright said that the allegations *did* concern the dark secrets of the "pamper parties," and that the women involved were determined, this time, to be heard.

Cartwright claimed that the girls "were invited to a party either by a friend or some of Nygard's affiliates, and at the party they in some cases were invited to his room to discuss modeling contracts."

"What they're alleging is that . . . they were sexually assaulted or raped by Mr. Peter Nygard," she continued.

The women had first made their complaints to the Bahamas police way back in July 2019, Cartwright said, and she insisted that despite years of struggle, they were still willing to fight: "They are resolute that they want justice, and that Mr. Nygard should be stopped."

Nygard's attorney Prober insisted that the investigation would go "nowhere, absolutely nowhere."

His spokesman, Ken Frydman, added that all of the new allegations were "false," and part of "a long-running malicious and vicious conspiracy dating back to at least as early as 2010 to pay off and coerce women to fabricate and manufacture sexual stories in an effort to destroy Nygard and his business."

Strangely, though, the normally pugnacious and PR-friendly Nygard was nowhere to be seen as one explosive story after another broke in early 2020. Meanwhile, the news out of his company was bleak—no matter how much spin they tried to put on it.

Almost immediately after the raid, Dillard's—one of Nygard's biggest American distributors—announced that they would no longer support his clothing lines. The statement read, "In light of the serious allegations concerning Peter Nygard, which are in direct opposition to our core values, Dillard's has refused current deliveries, canceled all existing orders and suspended all future purchases from Nygard." (As of mid-March 2020, however, his dedicated brand shop was still live on Dillards.com, featuring dozens of items for sale and no mention of the allegations against him.)

Just hours after that, Nygard's spokesman announced that the fashion designer was stepping down effective immediately as chairman of the Nygard Companies, and that he would even divest his ownership. Nygard made the difficult decision, he claimed, "recognizing the priority of the welfare of the thousands of Nygard employees, retail partners, loyal customers, vendors, suppliers, and business partners." (The statement did not mention how this move could benefit Nygard in his Jane Doe suit, where several of his companies are listed as defendants.)

The hits would keep on coming. On March 3, 2020, the CBC reported that Nygard had been slapped with legal action by Hollywood mega-mogul Mike Sitrick, the founder, chairman, and CEO of crisis PR agency Sitrick & Company. Sitrick alleged that Nygard hired him between 2014 and 2017 to help with his legal tussles in the Bahamas. According to Sitrick, Nygard skipped out on a $1.6 million bill.

A California arbitrator reviewed the case and found that although Nygard believed Sitrick "had over-billed him and he didn't get the 'bang for his buck,'" the fashion designer "was slow paying the bills and many times the amounts he paid didn't match the invoices sent." The arbitrator ordered Nygard to pay up in October 2018.

As of January 2020, Sitrick hadn't been able to track him down. So he got creative.

A private investigation team connected to Sitrick hired process server Liana Borisov to hunt Nygard. One tip they shared: Nygard liked to host rowdy parties at his Marina Del Rey home on Sundays, and he loved for gorgeous women to attend.

So, Borisov said in a court affidavit, she went to the property on November 10, 2019, dressed more "provocatively" than she normally would to deliver paperwork. It was all easier than she had expected.

"After entering the property I was greeted by a woman who told me she was 'checking people in' for Peter Nygard," Borisov said. "The woman asked me if I was 'one of the new girls.' The woman also told me that Peter Nygard was upstairs, preparing himself, and would be down soon. Other provocatively dressed females were waiting." In the process, Borisov was able to pass off her paperwork to an assistant, and she left before things got uncomfortable.

As of press time, though, he still hasn't paid.

Meanwhile, it seems Nygard's companies have been working overtime to free up cash. The CBC reported on March 3, 2020, that Nygard had secretly gotten a $50 million debenture (loan security agreement) in late 2019, secured by four of his company's properties—including his Winnipeg and Toronto headquarters.

Nygard's rep insisted that it was not a desperate cash grab; but rather, the decision of a savvy businessman.

"As a responsible owner of a company that just celebrated its 50th anniversary, Mr. Nygard of course has planned a successor program with the objective of enabling his key associates to end up as owners of the company," Ken Frydman said in a statement. "To that end, a new banking arrangement was arranged. The debenture is a normal security component of any financing." In all, he insisted it was a "normal business practice," and that there was "nothing out of the ordinary."

Only days later, though, there was more puzzling news from up north. The Nygard Group of Companies announced on March 10, 2020, that they would be filing "a notice of intention to file a proposal" under the Canadian Bankruptcy and Insolvency Act. According to Price Waterhouse Cooper Canada, a notice of intention (or "NOI") "allows financially troubled institutions to restructure their affairs." In addition, it allows the company "to avoid bankruptcy" by granting the company thirty days of protection from creditors once the NOI is filed. That period is often extended if the company in question can prove that they are working toward an equitable solution.

Indeed, Nygard's rep Frydman was bullish as he announced this latest change in a statement to the press.

"The fact that the company has made such a filing does not mean that the company is bankrupt," the statement read. "Rather, the company is committed to positioning itself for long-term financial stability and is developing a restructuring plan that is acceptable to the company's various stakeholders."

"In the interim," he insisted, "it's 'business as usual' at the company and at its retail stores."

That wasn't exactly true. On March 11, 2020, *Winnipeg Free Press* reporter Ryan Thorpe broke the explosive news that Nygard employees had been directed to begin preserving all internal documents.

According to Thorpe, all employees and staff received an ominous memo from Nygard General Counsel Abe Rubinfeld on February 26—one day after the FBI raid in New York.

"Until further notice, do not discard, delete, overwrite, alter, or destroy any relevant paper documents or other physical items, or alter or destroy electronically stored information," the memo announced. "Until further notice, suspend any document destruction policies, to the extent any such policies are in effect."

Rubinfeld warned, "Please note that failure to preserve these materials or any other materials that fall within the scope of any of the categories set forth above could be detrimental" to Nygard's "position with respect to the lawsuit."

In addition, he wrote, it also "could constitute obstruction of the investigation, and could result in, among other things, criminal prosecution and/or other sanctions, as well as financial penalties and termination of your employment."

Nygard's personal attorney said it was "standard procedure," much ado about nothing. It even represented, he claimed "an example of the full cooperation that Nygard and his companies are providing" investigators and attorneys in the Jane Doe suit.

Little did he know, Nygard's legal troubles were about to get even worse.

On March 13, 2020, a Canadian judge handed down a staggering demand for Nygard and his companies: They would have just seven days to pay back a $25 million loan owed to American lenders White Oak Financial LLC and Second Avenue Capital Partners, or face government takeover. The lenders had previously asked the court to put the companies into receivership (a Canadian concept that would allow the court to force Nygard to sell off assets to settle his debt).

The lenders were furious that Nygard got a reprieve, telling the court that his companies were headed for disaster. In a March 10 filing, they wrote that "The Nygard Group's wholesale business appears to be in freefall" following the FBI raid and Jane Doe suit.

Although they had previously advanced the company a loan of $27.8 million in late 2019, that deal had been contingent on Nygard hiring a financial adviser, they claimed. That never happened.

"Everything this company says they're going to do, they don't," White Oak attorney Marc Wasserman claimed in court on March 12. They alleged that Nygard honchos were rebuffing their requests for meetings, and that they had funded the company's last four payrolls just to keep everything limping along. White Oak said they had no idea how Nygard planned to pay his employees in the future.

The judge said in response that it would be "in the best interest of all the creditors" if Nygard was given a little more time to make good. Despite that, the judge had troubling news to share: "There is no evidence that Mr. Nygard has indeed resigned, and 100 percent of the shares of the Nygard Group" are still owned by him.

Indeed, a source close to Nygard confirmed at press time that he was hiding out in Canada, running the businesses from his Winnipeg home.

Meanwhile, Nygard himself has remained silent. Rather than engage with the ongoing PR crisis, his company PR Twitter account has continued to churn out "Did You Know?" type tidbits about their leading man that are almost too good to be true.

@PeterNygardPR wrote on February 20, days before the FBI raid, "From the start, Peter Nygard developed a reputation of being an honest broker who could be fully trusted. And that's the foundation his business was built on that allowed his exponential success."

On February 27, two days after the raid: "When you review the many charitable gifts Peter Nygard has given over all the years of his life, it's amazing to note the millions of dollars to organizations, athletes and individuals in medical crisis."

On March 12, the day his lenders tried to take over his company in court: "In 1994, Peter Nygard and his Mom, Hilkka, returned to his beloved Finland for a visit. He wanted to find a way to pay homage to the veterans of the Winter War in Finland."

That same day: "Peter Nygard made it possible for all the associates in his companies to become healthier & more fit. Every NYGARD location became equipped with a state of the art gym for associates to use. Each of the cafeterias were mandated to only serve healthy meals."

(They neglected to mention that Nygard also reportedly weighed his employees at meetings and posted everyone's current weight in the cafeteria. Whoever loses the most weight in a given period wins a trophy.)

In some ways, it seems, Nygard may have his head in the sand about the seriousness of what he's facing. One by one, though, the markers of his charmed life are falling down around him.

According to online records, Nygard sold his yacht, the *Lady Hilkka*, sometime after 2018, with an asking price of $449,000. Viking Hill, his first footprint in the Bahamas, is currently operating as a hostel that charges roughly $40 per night for a bunk bed. Nygard's daughter, Bianca—once the pretty princess of his entire empire—lives in a small apartment on-site. When we visited Nygard Cay for this book (beaches are public in the Bahamas) it looked more like a hazardous ruin than a party palace. Peeling paint, broken glass, and rusty wires are the only remnants of what Nygard once considered his castle.

Apparently, the curious can even spend the night on the property—if they aren't afraid of the ghosts that still linger. Nygard Cay is listed on Rentalo.com for an eye-watering price of roughly $35,000 per night. The listing promises "the trip of a lifetime." Requests for more information were not returned.

CHAPTER 12
ME TOO

I thought that it was normal . . .
—Courtney Stodden

By the time this book hits the shelves, there probably will be enough new developments regarding Peter Nygard for a whole additional chapter—or a sequel. Each day, it seems, brings another long-buried secret to light.

Just three days before the manuscript was submitted, model and singer-songwriter Courtney Stodden came forward with the courage to speak about her own experiences with Peter Nygard, in the hopes that it would give another victim the strength to speak out—or to carry on for one more day.

Stodden, now twenty-five, is no stranger to the dark side of Hollywood. At just sixteen, she married fifty-year-old *Green Mile* star Doug Hutchison after the two struck up a relationship online in 2011. Stodden's divorce from Hutchison was finalized on March 3, 2020.

Now, she is single and ready to talk about what she witnessed and experienced in her terrifying first years in Hollywood.

"Because I married into Hollywood, like the entire predatory vibe, I thought it was okay," she began. "I thought that it was normal."

Like so many others, though, Stodden experienced a whole new level of pain and freedom as the "Me Too" movement spread across America.

"You're reading about something, and you're like, 'I experienced that like this, the way they say it,'" she explained. "It's like, 'Well, I experienced that.' And then it's like, 'Oh my gosh.'"

"You sit with that for a while," she said. "And then I was just like, this isn't right. And then I replayed so many other predatorial experiences that I was a survivor of. And it's shocking."

One of those experiences, she claims, was at the hands of Peter Nygard. When the news about the lawsuit against him and the FBI raid broke, she was flooded with memories.

"My first reaction was like, 'Oh my God,'" she remembered. "And I sat on my bed and I was kind of playing through in my mind what happened."

Stodden had met Nygard at his 2014 Night of 100 Stars Oscar viewing party, when she was 19. The two posed for photos together on the red carpet. In them, Nygard can be seen cupping his hand tightly just below Stodden's breast.

"I was just replaying all of this stuff and then I thought to myself, 'Was that appropriate that he grabbed my chest and my ass?' You know, at the event and over my clothes, was that appropriate? The way he was kissing my neck. The way he was kissing, pulling me so close to him."

As with so many other victims, Nygard offered Stodden the keys to a career in fashion—if she'd only go along with his unspoken requirements.

Stodden recalled Nygard "promising me that he would help me with my clothing line that I wanted to work on at that time if I would just, you know, spend some time with him."

"He had like that spanx line [Nygard Slims] or whatever that was, and he was telling me, 'Oh, come model, you know, the Spanx for me! Then after that you're going to have to come to a pamper party and then you and I are going to escape on my boat to the island and then we're going to talk about your career there. But I can't have anybody else around.'"

As Nygard got handsy with her in the middle of a bustling red carpet, Stodden recalled, "Nobody said anything. Nobody said a thing. It was like, you know, 'Oh, you're so lucky to be standing next to this mogul, who's found the fountain of youth and can shower you with so much success.'"

Stodden managed to escape into the party, but Nygard wasn't letting her go so easily. She claims he launched an all-out campaign to get the teen down to Nygard Cay.

"He would text me almost every day, very explicit texts and you know, playing the power game with me," she said. "Unfortunately, I've had so many other men do that as well. I mean, there's a plethora of men in mind that I've done the same thing that he's done. I'm realizing now that it's so inappropriate, it's not right., And I remember thinking it was normal."

"That happened to me multiple times before Peter did that to me," Stodden continued. "So I think the first time that happened, I felt, 'This is an inappropriate thing.' But I think at that point in time when I met Peter, it was like, 'Oh cool.'"

"You know, it still hurt inside, but I was like, 'Oh, okay. Well this is part of the game, you know, it's the casting couch.' I mean, I wasn't going to ever sleep with him, but he could just touch me and do whatever he wanted when he was around me because he was helping me."

It was a tragically familiar path for Stodden, and she was heading right down it yet again.

"Thank God my mom intervened and basically stopped the process," she said. "Because I was three, two, one . . . getting ready to go down to that island and be raped."

Stodden explained, "I had called my mom and I said, 'Mom, you know Peter?' And she's like, 'Oh God. Yeah. What's going on?' And I said, 'Well, he's offering me clothing lines, harassing me to go to to his island.'"

"And so she ended up calling him for me and she said, 'You know, if you want to help her with her career, I'm going to be there with my daughter in person with her every second, even if it's out on that island. I'm going with her.' And he said, 'No, you're not. I can't have anybody else with her.'"

"And my mom was like, 'Well then she's not going and you're going to stop contacting my daughter.'"

Luckily, that was the end of it. Nygard moved on to other targets and left Stodden alone. She did attend his Night of 100 Stars Oscar party again in 2017, but this time he didn't pose with her at all on the carpet.

Today, Stodden is still chilled by the experience, but even more disturbed when she thinks about the other girls who didn't escape so easily.

"It's so scary 'cuz I was so young in this town and so naive and I can only imagine, you know, the damage that he's done to the girls that were a little bit more naive than me," she said. "Just, yeah . . . What a monster."

Seeing predators like Nygard shoved into the spotlight is bittersweet for women, like Stodden, who have been victimized by powerful men. The hope of justice is vindicating, but every new story has the potential to tear open old wounds.

Recording this interview just days after Harvey Weinstein was sentenced to twenty-three years in prison, Stodden was still reeling from the revelations of the recent months, Nygard included.

"I'm suffering from so much trauma that I can't even comprehend at this moment in time," she explained. "It's been really difficult growing up in this industry."

For Stodden, though, the courage of other victims like her is what ensures that men like Nygard will not succeed in silencing their darkest secrets.

"I spoke with Rose McGowan, and she's been really awesome," Stodden said. "There are plenty of other celebrity girlfriends that I have and we, and we talk about it."

"Even though I seem brave right now and I'm getting so many messages from women about how brave I am to be talking about this, and how grateful they are to me, I'm still learning," she continued. "There's certain things that I still have to speak out about and I'm not brave enough to write about them yet."

"So my experience is very fresh. My newfound freedom is very fresh. And, um, and yeah, and I'm, I'm grateful for women as yourself as well, you know, for helping women like myself along to, to feel like we're not alone. That's the most important."

***

For Reverend C. B. Moss, the community activist who watched women begin to step forward against Nygard in the Bahamas, it is the victims who deserve the credit for creating the new and better world that is hopefully unfolding.

"Well, women in the Bahamas are feeling empowered because they realize that they have a voice now," he said in an interview for this book. "Of course, time will strengthen that sense of empowerment. There may still be some [timidity] right now, but in time I think women are going to step forward and claim their full rights. But you can already feel it."

"Powerful men in particular will realize that they cannot continue to exploit women," he said, "particularly the more vulnerable ones who for psychological, financial, or other reasons, are very vulnerable to that kind of approach."

Ultimately, although the Nygard scandal has been a stain on the Bahamas, Moss said that all of the pain and heartbreak is giving way to a better world already.

"You know, this is good," he said. "It's good that we are opening up the can of worms as it relates to this kind of treatment of women."

"We hope that a lot of good will come out of this, even though it's a very tragic situation and our hearts go out to the alleged victims, particularly the, the juvenile ones, but still, hopefully some good will come out of it," he said. "We just hope that others will take note. And, on the other hand, if they do not desist, then we just hope that the law will be there to make them wish they did."

EPILOGUE

As the final chapters of this book came together, sources were sending last-minute information, court reporters were sending over final files, and final edits were being made. In the whirlwind of that period, news from the outside world intruded. The coronavirus descended, creating an atmosphere of doubt and fear around the world. Perhaps just as suddenly and shockingly, here in the United States, mega-producer and serial rapist Harvey Weinstein was sentenced to twenty-three years in prison.

It was a moment that many never thought would happen. After decades of crushing his vulnerable victims in a system of exploitation and abuse, Weinstein was finally called to account. The American justice system had—seemingly against all odds—worked. Weinstein's victims got to see justice served in a way that had eluded the many victims of Jeffrey Epstein.

Of course, it remained to be seen whether Weinstein would serve out his full sentence. Before the day of sentencing was even over, his lawyers were arguing for a reduced term. The producer's showy wielding of a walker and complaints about his health suggested that he might be angling for more of a "Club Fed" situation than the local Rikers Island or MCC (the site where Epstein took his last breaths). He claimed he was having heart problems.

Still, it was a victory—however small—and not just for his victims. The journalists and activists who worked for years to expose the truth about Weinstein could finally be validated by the fact that somebody had actually listened. Somebody actually cared that women's lives were being utterly destroyed, in the darkness.

It hasn't always felt that way.

Yet surely, none of us are naive enough to think that we've reached some new paradise of social justice for sexual assault victims. Despite trophies like the Weinstein verdict, an American is still sexually assaulted every seventy-three seconds. The problem with our culture goes far beyond the deeds of any one man.

***

At the time of this writing, Nygard had not been arrested or charged for anything related to the civil allegations against him. He continues to furiously deny all of the claims. You may already have passed your own verdict, but he remains truly innocent until proven guilty--at least according to the justice system.

With people's lives at stake, though, must we continue to wait for the justice system to be the ultimate arbiter of whose lives are worth attention? The concepts of innocent and guilty still have a place in this twisted world. Yet the reality is that most of the rapists, abusers, harassers, and creeps of the world will never be caught, let alone punished. For anyone who takes the time to think about it, it's overwhelming and discouraging. How can we ever stop it?

So many people have asked me that question in the wake of Epstein, Weinstein, and now the allegations against Mr. Nygard. I surely don't have all the answers. From where I stand, however, there's only one path toward a better world for all of us in this regard.

Listen to the stories of the people you might normally ignore. Don't look away and block your ears when they're unpleasant. Ask questions. Above all, keep looking for the answers.

AFTERWORD

Subsequent to her detailed investigative reporting on Jeffrey Epstein's suspicious suicide, Melissa Cronin, has authored another book of sexual abuse, this time committed by the wealthy freak, Peter Nygard. This book describes details straight from the victims of Peter Nygard, who, similar to Jeffrey Epstein, entertained politicians, corrupt law enforcement, and celebrities on his bizarre, amusement park-like property in the Bahamas.

The subject matter of this nonfiction book makes it a difficult read, as author Melissa Cronin vividly describes the gruesome details. But it is an extremely credible story about Peter Nygard's victims, and a window into his bizarre life. Cronin is the daughter of an experienced Special Agent of the FBI who would be proud of her efforts to expose the allegations of sexual abuse of minors by another wealthy man who displays traits of a sociopath.

The sociopathic traits as described by the victims include Nygard's shallow emotions, lack of remorse, need for stimulation, incapacity for love, and manipulative, pathological lying that continued for decades. The only way to experience this maniacal behavior is to read this well-written book.

As a retired FBI agent, who had much success investigating sophisticated, organized crime and political corruption based in NYC, I would expect the investigating agents' efforts to corroborate victims' statements in this book with evidence seized in recent search warrants executed by the FBI. These search warrants seized records at Peter Nygard facilities in both New York and California.

I would investigate these crimes as a violation of the Racketeer Influenced and Corrupt Organizations Act (RICO), a federal law originally designed to combat organized crime in the United States but applicable to all types of crimes. It provides for prosecution and civil penalties for racketeering activity performed as part of an ongoing criminal enterprise. Nygard's accomplices, who were described by victims as knowingly transporting and detaining victims for Nygard's sexual abuse, are exposed to violations of this law.

One of the victims, a teacher who claims being raped by Nygard when she was fifteen years old, maintained a personal diary that captures her rape at that time. The details of this diary should also be corroborated by a forensics examination.

I believe this book can assist with the process for the victims to obtain justice for the crimes committed by so many people who could not have the courage to say no to Nygard. The evidence secured by the FBI should include photos, videos, emails, flight ledgers, etc. The FBI could compel cooperation from close criminal associates with this evidence. If that occurs, a major storm is coming, and Nygard's days of walking between the raindrops of freedom and abuse will be coming to an abrupt end.

—Mike Campi
Former FBI special agent
March 2020

INDEX

A NOTE ABOUT
HOT BOOKS

The world is burning, and yet the firelight illuminates the way out. The times are dire, even catastrophic. Nonetheless we can sense a grand awakening, a growing realization all around the globe that "people have the power, to dream, to rule, to wrestle the world from fools" in the prophetic words of Patti Smith.

But in order to rouse ourselves from the nightmares that hold us in their grip, we need to know more about the forces that bedevil us, the structures of power that profit from humanity's exploitation and from that of the earth. That's the impetus behind Hot Books, a series that seeks to expose the dark operations of power and to light the way forward.

Skyhorse publisher Tony Lyons and I started Hot Books in 2015 because we believe that books can make a difference. Since then the Hot Books series has shined a light on the cruel reign of racism and police violence in Baltimore (D. Watkins' *The Beast Side*); the poisoning of U.S. soldiers by their own environmentally reckless commanding officers (Joseph Hickman's *The Burn Pits*); the urgent need to hold U.S. officials accountable for their criminal actions during the war on terror (Rachel Gordon's *American Nuremberg*); the covert manipulation of the media by intelligence agencies (Nicholas Schou's *Spooked*); the rise of a rape culture on campus (Kirby Dick and Amy Ziering's *The Hunting Ground*); the insidious demonizing of Muslims in the media and Washington (Arsalan Iftikhar's *Scapegoats*); the crackdown on whistleblowers who know the government's dirty secrets (Mark Hertsgaard's *Bravehearts*); the disastrous policies of the liberal elite that led to the triumph of Trump (Chris Hedges' *Unspeakable*); the American wastelands that gave rise to this dark reign (Alexander Zaitchik's *The Gilded Rage*); the energy titans and their political servants who are threatening human survival (Dick Russell's *Horsemen of the Apocalypse*); the utilization of authoritarian tactics by Donald Trump that threaten to erode American democracy (Brian Klaas's *The Despot's Apprentice*); the capture, torture, and detention of the first "high-value target" captured by the CIA after 9/11 (Joseph Hickman and John Kiriakou's *The Convenient Terrorist*); the deportation of American veterans (J Malcolm Garcia's *Without a Country*); and the ways in which our elections have failed, and continue to fail their billing as model democracy (Steven Rosenfeld's *Democracy Betrayed*). With recent titles, such as *The Case against Impeaching Trump* by Alan Dershowitz and *The Case for Impeaching Trump* by Elizabeth Hotzman, as well as *War with Russia?* by Stephen Cohen, *Midnight in Samarra* by Frank Gregory Ford and Eleanor Cooney, and *The Plot to Overthrow Venezuela* by Dan Kovalik, the series continues, going where few publishers dare.

Hot Books are packed with provocative information and points of view that mainstream publishers usually shy from. Hot Books are meant not just to stir readers' thinking, but to stir trouble.

Hot Books authors follow the blazing path of such legendary muckrakers and troublemakers as Upton Sinclair, Lincoln Steffens, Rachel Carson, Jane Jacobs, Jessica Mitford, I.F. Stone and Seymour Hersh. The magazines and newspapers that once provided a forum for this deep and dangerous journalism have shrunk in number and available resources. Hot Books aims to fill this crucial gap.

American journalism has become increasingly digitized and commodified. If the news isn't fake, it's usually shallow. But there's a growing hunger for information that is both credible and undiluted by corporate filters.

A publishing series with this intensity cannot keep burning in a vacuum. Hot Books needs a culture of equally passionate readers. Please spread the word about these titles—encourage your bookstores to carry them, post comments about them in online stores and forums, persuade your book clubs, schools, political groups and community organizations to read them and invite the authors to speak.

It's time to go beyond packaged news and propaganda. It's time for Hot Books . . . journalism without borders.

—David Talbot
Founder and former editor in chief, *Salon*